We the Who?

We the Who?

A Citizen's Manifesto on
America

Brett H. Lewis

iUniverse LLC
Bloomington

We the Who?
A Citizen's Manifesto on America

iUniverse books may be ordered through booksellers or by contacting:

iUniverse LLC
1663 Liberty Drive
Bloomington, IN 47403
www.iuniverse.com
1-800-Authors (1-800-288-4677)

ISBN: 978-1-4917-0869-9 (sc)
ISBN: 978-1-4917-0868-2 (hc)
ISBN: 978-1-4917-0867-5 (e)

Library of Congress Control Number: 2013917333

Printed in the United States of America

iUniverse rev. date: 11/20/2013

DISCLAIMERS

Documents, Lists, and Tables

With respect to documents, lists, and tables available from this book, the author and publisher do not make any warranty, express or implied, including the warranties of merchantability and fitness for a particular purpose, or assume any legal liability or responsibility for the accuracy, completeness, or usefulness of any information, apparatus, product, or process disclosed.

Reference from this book to any entity, product, service, or information does not constitute an endorsement or recommendation by the author or publisher, and is provided with the intent of providing information only.

Internet

Because of the dynamic nature of the Internet, any web addresses or links contained in this book may have changed since publication and may no longer be valid.

Opinions and Views

The opinions and views expressed in this book are those of the author and do not necessarily reflect the opinions and views of the publisher. Examples of analysis performed within this book are for illustrative purposes only. They should not be utilized in real-world analytic products as they are based only on very limited and dated open source information. Assumptions made within the analysis are not necessarily reflective of the position of the publisher.

We the Who? is dedicated to we the people who have made and will continue to make the United States of America the greatest country in the world. It is also dedicated to Americans who will not speak out for fear that no one will listen to or care about what they have to say. Stand up and exercise your constitutional right to be heard because, in America, a citizen's voice can truly have the power of Joshua's horn.

CONTENTS

ACKNOWLEDGMENTS

First and foremost: many thanks to God for watching over me and to my family for their love and support.

A special thanks to my daughter Nicole and friends Beverly Foster and Richard Hammond for their review of my drafts, feedback, and other invaluable contributions relevant to the subjects discussed in *We the Who?*, and to Sheldon Laskin who provided interpretations of legal phraseology and court rulings.

Thanks to Trinity United Methodist Church in Highland Park, New Jersey, for giving me a lasting religious foundation and sense of belonging during my days as an adolescent. To my classmates from the Edison High School Class of 1969 in Edison, New Jersey, for their support and friendship during my high school years, support and friendship that continues to this day. During the 1960s, when racial and civil unrest were at a peak, Trinity United Methodist Church and Edison High School typified how America should be—a nation where skin color does not matter.

To my barbers, Rev. Nathanial Sanders and his son Dwayne, for refreshing debates. Dwayne learned how to keep me quiet while he was making a point. He starts trimming my mustache and takes his time doing it, thus reinforcing an important principle in effective communication—a good communicator must first be quiet and listen before speaking.

Last, but not least, to the United States of America for assuring and protecting the rights, freedom, and security I enjoy. God Bless America!

INTRODUCTION

During the HBO movie *The Tuskegee Airmen*, an African American US Army Air Corps officer expressed to a US Senate committee his frustration with the discriminatory treatment of African American fighter pilots during World War II:

> As a United States Army Officer who gladly puts his life on the line every day, there's no greater conflict within me. How do I feel about my country? And how does my country feel about me? Are we only to be Americans when the mood suits you? (Braugher 1995)

Echoing this sentiment as an African American US Army veteran who would also put his life on the line to defend America, *how do I feel about my country and how does my country feel about me?* Am I an expendable pawn in a political chess match to be nurtured only during elections or when the mood suits my elected leaders? Do other Americans share my concerns?

America was formed based on a vision of democracy where supreme power is supposed to be vested in the people—a vision reinforced by President Lincoln, in his historic Gettysburg Address, when he stated "that this nation, under God, shall have a new birth of freedom and that government of the people, by the people, for the people, shall not perish from the earth."

In addition to Lincoln's proclamation, America's guiding principles and tenets of democracy are embodied in the US Constitution and Declaration of Independence—both defining America's ethos and path to continued greatness, and our collective identity as "we the people." However, are Americans losing sight of who we the people are, or more importantly, who we need to be in order for America to continue as the greatest of nations? To ensure that government of the people, by the people, and for the people shall not perish from the earth, we the people need to be awake, alert, and aware. *Are we?*

A fictional television news anchor delivered a prophetic tirade about America in the 1976 movie *Network*. If you saw the movie, you may remember these excerpts:

> Everybody's out of work or scared of losing their job. . . . we
> sit watching our TVs while some local newscaster tells us that
> today we had fifteen homicides and sixty-three violent crimes,
> as if that's the way it's supposed to be . . . I don't know what
> to do about the depression, and the inflation, and the Russians,
> and the crime in the street . . . *I'm mad as hell, and I'm not
> going to take this anymore!* (Finch 1976, italics mine)

Replace "depression" with "recession"; "the Russians" with "Afghanistan," "North Korea," "Syria," or "Iran"; and "inflation" with "unemployment"; this outburst could hold just as true today as it did in 1976. If so, getting "mad as hell" would be the first step necessary to regain our collective identity and ensure America's continued greatness. The next step would be to do something about it.

I am not a scholar or journalist, nor a political, economic, or legal pundit. I am a sixtyish self-employed middle-class American citizen who cannot afford private health insurance (thank God for VA health benefits). I live in suburbia in a mortgage-free home with a paid-for late-model car, and I am currently receiving Social Security benefits and a meager monthly stipend from my savings. To date, I am fortunate that my only ongoing financial burdens are monthly living expenses and taxes. The 2008 recession and being a full-time family caregiver for a year wreaked havoc on my financial stability; both events resulted in my need to work beyond the traditional retirement age of sixty-five.

As a left-of-center Independent, my political inclinations span conservative and liberal ideologies. I am a divorced grandfather who will soon be eligible for Medicare, if it still exists, and a by-product of the Civil Rights era. I am a protestant Christian, pro-choice, and ambivalent about same-sex marriage. I support a one-time amnesty for in-country illegal immigrants, the death penalty with reservations, and a flat federal income tax rate for all Americans. I oppose sin taxes and government intrusions into my privacy and how parents should raise their children. I do not oppose gun-control regulation that does not infringe on my Second Amendment rights. I preferred the "public option" proposal for health care reform can support the compromise known as Obamacare. Lastly, I support the need to maintain a superior military capability.

In *We the Who?,* I will expose you to a series of short essays on a variety of issues, drawing my conclusions from history, logic, social inclinations, religious beliefs, and personal experiences. This is not a scholarly work written in eloquent prose from comprehensive and unimpeachable professional-level research, interviews with subject-matter experts or pundits, or with a high level of literary acumen. I wrote subjectively, from my heart, and whether my writing is incisive and articulate or not, or my analysis is accurate or not, or my conclusions and recommendation well-founded or not, *We the Who?* is a peek into my evolving body of knowledge and life experiences as an American citizen.

You may or may not agree with my opinions and conclusions, and your personal or family circumstances may be better, worse, or the same as mine; however, we are the same American citizens with expectations and aspirations. We are all looking for the light at the end of the American Dream tunnel, a light that has become increasingly difficult to find over the past several years. Even though I currently have a morose view of America, I maintain an optimistic outlook and will continue to hold my elected representatives accountable for putting America on the path to a more prosperous future.

During the 2008 presidential campaign, then–US Senator Obama's campaign motto was "Yes We Can." Yes, we definitely can, but it is now 2013, and Americans need to get it done so we can proclaim "Yes We Did" and I can stop asking the question "We the Who?"

By the time *We the Who?* is published, future domestic and global events may alter some of my thinking; however, right or wrong, this is a citizen's manifesto on America as of October 2013.

Let's begin . . .

Chapter 1

CLASSISM AND RACISM

There's no greater conflict within me.

Bitter debates about classism were at their height during the 2008 recession, especially when individual pension, investment, and retirement packages were being drained while corporate and Wall Street executives continued to receive exorbitant compensation and golden parachute severance packages while millions of rank-and-file employees were being discharged en masse, home foreclosures were at a record high, the automobile industry was close to bankruptcy, and major banking institutions were failing. As the recession receded and the economy began a slow recovery, rich-versus-poor sentiments also mellowed; however, the debates continued in areas such as corporate executive greed and taxing the rich at higher federal income tax rates.

On the other side of the coin, racism has morphed into a covert and institutionally malevolent form since the 1960s, and is still as pervasive and debilitating as ever. Granted, the racial climate in America has improved as compared to the days of Jim Crow, but remember that some poisonous snakes appear to be smiling before they strike. Some of these snakes have interesting names, such as colorism, the n-word, and voter suppression.

Another insidious "ism" is sexism. As a male, I cannot appropriately convey the frustration felt by women when confronted with sexism's crippling effects. Therefore, I will not discuss sexism in *We the Who?*; however, sexism is another poisonous snake that needs to be defanged.

Since classism and racism are deep-rooted facts of life, I will discuss several topics that I believe paint a clear picture of these "isms" in America:

—Classism

- En Masse Employee Layoffs
- Executive Greed
- Should the Rich Pay More Taxes?

—Racism

- Barack Obama and Other Victims
- Colorism
- New N-Words
- Sandy Hook and Chicago: A Tale of Two Cities
- Voter Suppression
- Wealth, Power, and "Forty Acres and a Mule"
- Who Controls the Fountains?
- Zimmerman: The Last Straw?

Classism

Is America divided into two economic classes of haves and have-nots? Lynari Morales asked this question in the Gallup article *Fewer Americans See U.S. Divided into Haves, Have-Nots*. The answer surprised me. After the 2008 recession, I thought most Americans recognized the class division between the haves and have-nots. Apparently, I was wrong. In mid-2011, 41 percent said "Yes, divided," and 58 percent said "No, not divided." To explain, Morales wrote:

> Americans' views of their own position as "haves" or "have-nots" have been remarkably stable, even as the nation's economic problems have intensified. Still, the finding that fewer Americans now than in 2008 consider U.S. society as divided into "haves" and "have-nots" suggests a decreasing, rather than increasing, level of worry about unfair income distribution in the U.S. at this time. (Morales 2011)

However, there has been a steady increase of Americans who are in the have-nots category, indicative of a decrease in the distribution of wealth to the middle class and poor. As a member of the middle class, I am concerned about this inequity and the behaviors of the top 1 percent of the "haves."

Focusing on the top 1 percent of the haves (super-rich corporate and Wall Street executives) and the rich in general, two stories emerge. The former is a tale of greed and financial gluttony, and the latter a tale of unfair stereotypes and taxation. In this regard, my concerns are (1) the en masse discharge of employees by corporate and Wall Street executives who protect their own security with disproportionate compensation packages and golden parachutes and (2) income tax legislation requiring the rich to pay income taxes at a higher federal tax rate than lower-income taxpayers.

En Masse Employee Layoffs

Executive and rank-and-file employees should equally incur the consequences of company failures as well as the benefits of success and profits. In other words, the needs of the "many" rank-and-file employees should equal the needs of the executive "few" with *all* having the same opportunities in their collective pursuit of happiness. However, as evidenced by frequent en masse layoffs, the needs of executives seem to outweigh the needs of all other employees. This said, I concede there will be situations, such as the potential insolvency of a business, when en masse layoffs are a last resort; however, this should not occur without legal oversight. Currently, the only restrictive requirement is the Worker Adjustment and Retraining Notification Act that requires all companies with over a hundred employees to give a sixty-day notice of an en masse layoff (Department of Labor).

Without considering union contracts, the following recommendations could provide the suggested oversight:

- Mandate the creation of a federal business court and expand existing state business court systems to all states, with the legal authority to allow or disallow the en masse discharge of employees. If an en masse layoff is approved, confirm the appropriate number to be discharged to ensure a company's solvency. If a company offers severance packages for voluntary discharges (financial incentives for employees to voluntarily quit), this action would be exempt from business court approval.

- Based on the total number of employees, establish a threshold percentage of discharged employees that would be considered an en masse layoff and trigger a business court review. To prevent companies from conducting multiple layoffs over a short period of time with each below the threshold percentage, set appropriate time constraints. For example, if the layoff threshold were 1 percent of total employees and a company conducted two nonreviewable layoffs of a half percent each, any future layoffs for the next five years would require a business court review. In other words, a company cannot lay off more than 1 percent of their total workforce during any five-year period.
- If the layoffs affected one state or multiple states, state and federal business courts would have jurisdiction, respectively. Appeals of a business court decision would be expeditiously handled by the appropriate state or federal courts of appeal.

Regarding the aforementioned business court requirement, there is precedent for this approach. Title 11 (Bankruptcy) of the United States Code specifies time limits on when someone can file again for bankruptcy protection, and the court will review multiple filings and deny those it believes are an abuse of the code. The court must also approve the terms of any bankruptcy. For corporations, the rules are different. There are virtually no restraints on how many times a corporation can file for bankruptcy protection or the length of time between corporate Chapter 11 filings; however, the court must approve the terms of all corporate bankruptcy filings.

Regardless of whether or not my suggestions are feasible, changes are needed. En masse layoffs should be a last resort and, without regulation, will continue with impunity. All Americans have the unalienable rights of life, liberty, and the pursuit of happiness, and earning a living is definitely a critical component of the pursuit of happiness. Accordingly, companies should be required to show cause in court before executing en masse layoffs.

Executive Greed

In 1787, Thomas Jefferson wrote:

> It seems to be the law of our general nature, in spite of individual exceptions; and experience declares that man is the only animal which devours his own kind, for I can apply no milder term to the governments of Europe, and to the general prey of the rich on the poor. (Jefferson 1787)

As an example, greed is a ravenous enabler of classism and a defect within our economic system that enables the preying on others who are not wealthy or powerful. In order to understand this better, look no further than the greed of corporate and Wall Street executives and their credo as articulated by fictional corporate raider Gordon Gekko in the 20th Century Fox movie *Wall Street*, who says, "Greed, for lack of a better word, is good. Greed is right. Greed works. Greed clarifies, cuts through, and captures the essence of the evolutionary spirit" (Douglas, *Wall Street,* 1987). One of the ancient Dead Sea Scrolls, the War Scroll, expressed a more appropriate credo: "Every creature of greed shall wither quickly away like a flower at harvest time" (WildBranch Ministry).

On many occasions, corporate executives proclaim that employees are a company's most valuable asset. In my opinion, the mantra is that executives are the most valuable assets and rank-and-file employees are the most expendable commodities or, more accurately, corporate chattel—quintessential classism. I am reminded of a defense proffered by Al Pacino, in the Universal Studios movie *Scent of a Woman*, while defending a friend. "He won't sell anybody out to buy his future," he says, "and that, my friends, is called integrity. Now that's the stuff leaders should be made of" (Pacino 1992).

Can the same be said about corporate and Wall Street executives who lay off employees en masse while reaping the benefits of exorbitant compensation packages and are contractually protected by extravagant golden parachute severance packages? According to a report by Governance Metrics International (GMI), a corporate governance consultancy, many golden parachutes are so large that they seem to be only in the interests of the departing executives. The report lists twenty-one CEOs whose golden parachutes are worth more than the average US worker would make in forty-nine lifetimes. In the case of General Electric's former CEO, John Welch Jr., the figure is $417 million, or 203 lifetimes for the average American worker. Another example is Viacom's former CEO, Thomas Freston, who worked for only one year and received a $100 million-plus golden parachute (Harkinson 2012).

Executives are expected to be the highest-paid employees because most are custodians of millions or billions of dollars of assets and have fiduciary or profit-and-loss (P&L) responsibilities. With some exceptions, most nonexecutive employees do not carry a fiduciary or P&L burden. However, from the CEO to the lowest-ranking worker, *all* are employees of the company and, with the exception of the exempt or nonexempt employee status regarding overtime pay, the mechanism by which terms of employment and compensation are established should be the same for all employees based on rank and time of employment. To explain this concept further, let's examine the military compensation model.

Military compensation is based on a graduated pay scale determined by rank and time of service, not individually negotiated contracts as is the case with many corporate and Wall Street executives. Enlisted service members and officers can look at their respective pay scales and know exactly what their monthly base pay will be—no exceptions. Good performance is rewarded by recognition, awards, medals, and promotions—not monetary bonuses. Lastly, service members are eligible for full retirement benefits after twenty years of service and are all subject to the same formulae to determine retirement pay—set percentages of their monthly base pay based on rank and length of service at retirement.

The military also has predetermined perks based on rank or assigned duty. For example, service members of any rank can receive additional hazardous-duty pay if assigned to a combat zone or explosive ordinance disposal, jump pay if required to parachute, and so on. Also, the military awards one-time signing bonuses to entice enlistment or reenlistment for service in critically short skill sets. The type of authorized military housing is determined by rank and marital status. General officers in designated positions warrant the assignment of officer aide-de-camps and enlisted aides, chauffeured transportation, and the like. Unlike corporate and Wall Street America, all military perks end upon leaving the service, and there are no negotiated golden parachute packages.

Returning to corporate and Wall Street America, as explained in an excerpt from a Western Washington University journalism paper entitled *America's Rich Get Richer*, compensation is disproportionately skewed in favor of executives:

> The December 21, 2011, *Seattle Times* . . . noted that average U.S. household income increased sixty-two percent between 1969 and 2007, but income for the top one percent rose more than 300 percent.

> Paul Krugman [Nobel Prize-winning economist and *New York Times* columnist] noted in November 2011 that all American redistribution of income away from the bottom eighty percent has gone to the highest income one percent and that a report looking only through 2005 found that almost two-thirds of the rising share of top one percent income went to the top 0.1 percent (the richest one-thousandth), who saw their income rise more than 400 percent from 1979 to 2005. (Western Washingtom University 2012)

Earnings for production and nonsupervisory workers, who comprise about 80 percent of the private nonfarm workforce, have risen just over 6.2 percent since June 2009, and consumer prices have risen nearly 7.2 percent. Adjusted for inflation, wages have fallen 0.8 percent, yet executive compensation remains at astronomically high levels (Wiseman 2012). For additional perspective, let's look at the current CEO-to-worker pay ratio:

> The ratio of CEO-to-worker pay has increased 1,000 percent since 1950, according to data from Bloomberg. Today Fortune 500 CEOs make 204 times regular workers on average, Bloomberg found. The ratio is up from 120–1 in 2000, 42–1 in 1980 and 20–1 in 1950. (Huffington Post 2013)

To level the playing field and take greed out of the equation, consider a compensation model that includes these components:

- If executives warrant employment contracts, so do all employees. Otherwise, eliminate employment contracts.
- As in the military, establish a graduated pay scale for management and nonmanagement employees based on rank and time of employment. Management and nonmanagement employees would be analogous to military officers and enlisted personnel, respectively.
- Eliminate golden parachute packages. Executives should be subject to the same severance criteria as all other employees (i.e., salary and benefits based on time of employment and rank).
- Implement mandatory profit sharing, which could be a combination of cash and stock, as appropriate. Other retirement and investment options, such as 401(k)s, savings accounts, or IRAs, can be offered as discretionary additions.
- Unlike the military, maintain monetary bonus systems based on performance. For example, if, as part of a bonus, executives get additional stock options as a percentage of their salaries, all employees should enjoy the same stock options as a percentage of their respective salaries.
- Eliminate non-business-related perks, but as in the military, maintain a consistent set of basic perks available to all employees based on their job description and disruptions to personal and family life, such as business travel requirements and personal security needs.
- Discontinue perks after an employee leaves the employment of the company.

There is one scenario not addressed in the above suggestions. In the military, enlisted and officer positions are filled from within among personnel that started their careers at the lowest officer or enlisted ranks, starting at an age that allows for twenty years of service (the minimum full-retirement threshold). The exceptions are medical doctors, chaplains, and attorneys, who receive direct commissions as captains. However, in corporate and Wall Street America, many senior executives are hired from outside the company and, because of their age when hired, will not be able to accrue the time of employment necessary for traditional early or full retirement; however, this should not be an issue. The exorbitant levels of executive compensation should be more than enough to overcome the financial impacts of not being eligible for a company's retirement plan. If an executive chooses to leave one company to join another, voluntarily chooses to stop working, or reaches a mandated retirement age, it is done at his or her own risk. This is the way it is for lower-level employees. Executives should not be treated any differently, but that is usually not the case, especially when executive golden parachute packages are involved.

The current justification for lavish executive compensation and severance packages is that they are needed for a company to remain competitive in obtaining and retaining the best executive talent. In principle, this is understandable, because this rationale is the same for the compensation received by marquee MLB, NFL, NBA, and other professional athletes. However, the NBA and NFL have salary caps limiting the amount of money teams can spend on players' salaries, and the MLB has a luxury tax on player compensation over a certain amount. Corporate and Wall Street America have no such restrictions, and that is the problem.

Jack Welch Jr. received a guaranteed $417 million golden parachute package equaling $21 million for each of his twenty years of service at GE. This package included the use of a luxury apartment, courtside or box seats to NFL and MLB games, seating at the US Open and Wimbledon tennis tournaments, country club fees, personal security services, corporate jet, cars, and restaurant bill reimbursement. Excessive would be a very polite descriptor of this package, and unfortunately, similar executive compensation packages are repeated throughout corporate and Wall Street America. GE justified Welch's golden parachute by stating that GE's market value increased by billions of dollars during Welch's tenure (CNN Money 2002). Fair enough, but what about the GE employees that worked with Welch? What compensation and perks did they receive?

At least Welch worked for a respectable period of time as a CEO. After a corporate merger, William Johnson became CEO of Duke Energy, yet the Board of Directors decided he was not right for the job. After three days as CEO, Johnson resigned with a severance package worth $44.4 million (Wile 2012). The right to profit from successful business endeavors is an integral part of the American Dream; however, corporate executives are disproportionately reaping the profits earned from the sweat and toil of all other employees. Again, keep in mind—a

$44.4 million severance package *for three days of work*—prototypical greed.

It may appear I am advocating collective bargaining, the current means by which unionized employees negotiate levels of pay, terms of employment, and retirement benefits, as a solution—not true. Managers and supervisors are not protected by the National Labor Relations Act, cannot join unions, and cannot be part of a bargaining unit (Repa). Therefore, collective bargaining would not fit with my vision of equitable compensation for all employees.

When economic conditions warranted such an action, various industries were regulated by the government, as was the airline industry until its deregulation in 1978. This may not pass a constitutional review, but it may be time for government regulation of executive compensation. After all, despite Gekko's claim that greed is good: "For what shall it profit a man, if he shall gain the whole world, and lose his own soul?" (Mark 8:36, King James Version).

Should the Rich Pay More Taxes?

Even though I criticized wealthy corporate and Wall Street executives, my answer is unequivocally *no*. I struggled with whether to discuss this issue in this chapter or chapter 2, "Socioeconomic," because executive greed and taxation of the rich are two totally different debates. Taxation is clearly an economic discussion, but the underlying emotional sentiments sparked by this subject arise from a class-oriented struggle resulting in debates and reactions more akin to class warfare than economic discourse. As such, this discussion would be better served in this chapter.

To avert the 2013 "fiscal cliff," President Obama signed legislation that continued America's graduated federal income tax rates and raised rates on individuals making $250,000 or more a year. I disagreed with both actions. The rich should not have to pay taxes at a higher rate than everyone else and should not be penalized for wealth obtained while legitimately reaping the benefits of the American Dream. America needs to shift to a flat federal income tax where all Americans pay the same percentage of income taxes. Additionally, the 71,000-plus page US

Internal Revenue Code needs a complete overhaul. These are suggestions to consider:

- Establish a flat income tax rate for all forms of individual income such as salary/wages/tips, capital gains, dividends, and interest. This approach would be consistent with the Constitution's intent on providing equal rights for all Americans and removing the discriminatory nature of graduated tax rates.
- Lower the corporate tax rate. This would encourage continued job creation and jumpstart corporate investment in America's infrastructure. Also, consider raising the corporate tax rate to the same rate as the flat individual income tax over a ten-year period, resulting in a flat tax rate for both individuals and corporations.
- To mitigate the effect of a flat income tax rate, eliminate tax shelters, loopholes, and extraneous tax deductions. For the benefit of the middle class and poor, maintain the Earned Income Credit and deductions such as family/dependents, mortgage interest, sales and property taxes, as well as health care, job hunting, and education-related costs.

During the 2012 Republican presidential primaries, Mitt Romney was criticized for being "super-rich" and out of touch with lower-income Americans. Romney's gaffes, such as betting fellow candidate Rick Perry $10,000 during a debate, revealing that his wife drives two Cadillac cars, and stating that he has friends that are (rich) NASCAR team owners provided the fuel for criticism from his opponents throughout the primaries. In spite of this criticism, the wealthy should not be vilified, apologize for, or feel guilty about legitimately earned wealth or have to pay taxes at a higher tax rate because, again, they were extremely successful in achieving the American Dream. This would be tantamount to stereotyping the wealthy because of their class status, which, in my opinion, is no different than stereotyping individuals because of their religion, sexual persuasion, or race.

Romney, with a net worth over $200 million, qualified for a 15 percent federal income tax rate because a majority of his income was from capital gains. In 2011, capital gains were taxed at a maximum rate of 15 percent. Romney was stigmatized for supposedly taking unfair advantage of the tax system; however, he did nothing illegal, because the US tax code legally placed Romney in the 15 percent tax bracket.

Albert Einstein once said, "You have to learn the rules of the game. And then you have to play better than anyone else" ("Albert Einstein Quotes"). Einstein's rule applies to everyone, regardless of whether one is rich, middle class, or poor, especially when "playing the game" of federal, state, or local income taxes. If I became wealthy, I would be inclined to "play the game" by looking for the same legal tax deductions, shelters, and loopholes in the US tax code that the wealthy take advantage of to lower their tax burden.

In closing, since I am not an economist, I cannot begin to fathom the impact or practicality of my recommendations to mitigate the impacts of classism. Again, my main points are that the US tax code needs an overhaul and that all Americans should be subject to the same federal income tax rate. Additionally, targeting the wealthy for income tax increases and en masse layoffs for rank-and-file employees while executives protect and enrich themselves are discriminatory and class-oriented penalties that violate a main tenet of democracy—equality for all.

Unfortunately, classism does not operate alone. Combined with racism, it forms a formidable systemic and institutional hammer with classism as the handle and racism as the destructive head: a hammer that continually attempts to pound African Americans and other Americans of color into cultural submission and total disenfranchisement from the fruits of the American Dream. Having discussed the handle, let's examine the hammer's head.

Racism

Of all the "isms" in American society, racism impacted me the most; however, my experiences paled in comparison to what other African Americans endured during the days of Jim Crow. Since I cannot speak to the experiences of others, to provide context and put a human face to this discussion, I will share some of my family's experiences with racism.

My first memories of racism were as a child. While driving through Virginia, my parents and I were stopped by the police because my mother looked white and my father was black. At that time, interracial marriage was illegal under Virginia's antimiscegenation laws. After realizing my mother was black, the police officers cautioned us about continued travel in Virginia. Another experience was in New Jersey when my parents, sister, and I went to a restaurant for dinner, and we were ushered into an empty dining room. We could see white diners eating in a separate dining room that had plenty of empty tables.

While a high school senior, I applied for entrance into the United States Military Academy (commonly known as West Point). Even though I had a very competitive résumé, my guidance counselor unsuccessfully tried to steer me to other colleges. He felt my chances for selection were poor because West Point historically accepted very few black candidates. He unknowingly propagated the stereotype that African Americans were not smart or "good" enough to be accepted into prestigious white institutions such as West Point. Contrary to my guidance counselor's concerns, I was accepted into West Point.

After leaving active military service in 1981, I joined Procter and Gamble (P&G) as a manager and learned firsthand about racism in corporate America. When I was hired, out of 120-plus P&G executives worldwide, none were African American. During my thirteen-year tenure at P&G, one African American was finally promoted to vice president. On a more contemporary note, as of the end of 2012, there were only six African American CEOs of Fortune 500 companies.

At the grassroots level, in July 2012, an African American couple, Charles and Te'Andrea Wilson, were to be married in a predominantly white church in Mississippi, but the day before the wedding, the pastor canceled the wedding. Charles Wilson explained: "The church congregation had decided no black could be married at that church, and that if he went on to marry her, then they would vote [the pastor] out the church" (Huffington Post 2012). In May 2013, the tomb of African American actor Michael Clarke Duncan was desecrated by a vandal who put a black-faced caricature that resembled "Sambo" (an offensive depiction of a black person) on the tomb (TMZ 2013).

Since racism in America is so obvious and pervasive, it requires no further introduction.

Barack Obama and Other Victims

—**Barack Obama**

Because of death threats, then–US Senator Obama was assigned US Secret Service protection during the 2008 Democratic presidential primaries. It was the earliest the Secret Service had ever provided protection to a presidential candidate. In 2009, Barack Obama became the first African American president of the United States and has since been the victim of other historic "firsts."

During his first term of office, President Obama was barraged with what could be characterized as racist diatribe disguised as political discourse. For example, during a 2011 speech before Congress, Representative Joe Wilson, a white Republican from South Carolina, publically called President Obama a liar by shouting "You lie!" during Obama's speech before Congress. Would a white president have been publically "called out" while delivering a speech before Congress? This had never happened before, and according to the Office of the House Historian, Wilson was the only House member ever admonished for inappropriately speaking out while a president was delivering a speech. Most Republicans voted against admonishing Wilson, and after apologizing Wilson received numerous campaign donations and was a frequent guest at Republican fundraisers (CBS News 2010). Additionally, in 2011, Republican Speaker of the House John Boehner refused President Obama's request to speak before a joint session of Congress. The Senate Historical Office knows of no instance when Congress refused a presidential request to speak before a joint session of Congress (Foster 2011).

In 2012, when President Obama apologized for the inadvertent burning of several Qurans by the US military in Afghanistan, Republicans lashed out by labeling him as a president who made America weaker because Afghanistan President Karzai did not apologize for the murder of two army officers in an Afghan government facility (Cafferty 2012). On the other hand, President G. W. Bush apologized for the abuse of prisoners at the Abu Ghraib prison in Iraq, yet there was no corresponding Iraqi apology for the death and public desecration of four American security contractors in Iraq. With the exception of Democrats demanding the resignation of then–Secretary of Defense Donald Rumsfeld, negative political reactions toward Bush were mild

(FoxNews.com 2004). As a final example, I thought the "birther" challenges to President Obama's US citizenship were unique to him and racially motivated. The latter may still be true, but I discovered that white politicians, such as President Chester Arthur and US Senator Barry Goldwater, had their US citizenship challenged during their political careers ("Natural-Born-Citizen Clause of the U.S. Constitution").

President Obama has been criticized for sounding professorial and conveying a smug and elitist attitude. President Obama can sometimes sound like a preacher delivering a sermon, but I also see a president who is calm under pressure, articulate, well informed, and confident while communicating—qualities that should be present in all leaders. As far as I am concerned, if President Obama were white and named Barry O'Bannon, he would not have received this criticism. Sadly, many African Americans have to contend with similar stereotypes. *DiversityInc* magazine highlights two such stereotypes (DiversityInc):

- **"You are very articulate" or "You speak really well."**

   A compliment may have been intended, but these comments are insulting and condescending by implying the person being complimented (usually of person of color) is an exception to the rule and is exhibiting a speaking style atypical of his or her ethnic background. In other words, the underlying stereotype is that African Americans are not expected to be articulate or capable of speaking the "King's/Queen's English."

- **"You did not sound black over the phone."**

   How are African Americans supposed to sound? I am always amused when someone meets me for the first time. The look of surprise on his or her face is priceless when they see I am black because, on the phone, I sounded white.

To further amplify this point, when comments US Senator Harry Reid made in 2008 were publicized in 2010, he had to apologize for saying the race of then–US Senator Obama, whom he described as a "light-skinned" African American "with no Negro dialect, unless he wanted to have one," would help rather than hurt Obama's 2008 presidential bid (Elliot 2010). Even though he was being supportive of Obama, Reid's comments unfortunately added credence to discriminatory practices where a light-skinned African American, who is articulate "with no Negro dialect," is viewed more favorably and afforded more privileges than those who are dark-skinned and sound black. However, being viewed more favorably does not necessarily translate into being treated more favorably.

The opposing political party's criticism of and posturing against a sitting president is not new and "comes with the territory." Regarding President Obama, behaviors of the political opposition have been petty and vitriolic, all contributing to the gridlock that plagues our government and the perception that nothing gets done in Washington. Add racism to the hyper-partisan divisiveness that has become a prominent part of American politics, and this is a recipe for ineffective governance. In this regard, Nsenga Burton, *The Root*'s editor-at-large, pulled no punches:

> Racists have officially lost their minds. In recent weeks, the venom spewed at President Barack Obama would leave one to believe that we are in the midst of a racist renaissance . . . For some reason, some people are so enraged by how this country is purportedly being run that they cannot separate a real critique of the president's decisions from mean-spirited name-calling related to his race . . . Elected officials have reduced themselves to behaving like petulant children, storming in and out of meetings, and running to the media to lob personal attacks at the president, then offering lame apologies shortly afterward. (Burton 2011)

This racist venom spilled over into mainstream America. A Georgia bar owner posted two racist signs on his property. In 2009, he posted "Obama's plan for health-care: nigger-rig it." In 2012, the same bar owner posted "I do not support the nigger in the White House" (Kimble 2012).

As the last of many examples, the owner of a New Jersey business dressed a monkey figurine in an anti-Obama T-shirt and displayed it in front of his business (Star-Ledger Continuous News Desk 2012). By comparison, during the presidency of white presidents, how many "I do not support the honky in the White House" signs were posted on

African American properties? ("Honky" is a racial slur used by African Americans to describe white people.)

Returning to the political arena, let's examine Romney's criticism that President Obama failed to effectively work with Congress while Romney was able to do so with a majority-white Democratic Massachusetts legislature when he was governor. Romney conveniently omitted mention of Obama or Democratic-sponsored legislation that Republicans filibustered in Congress—over twenty bills and counting. The Republicans even filibustered or blocked Obama-nominated federal appointees and health care legislation (9/11 Health and Compensation Act) for 9/11 responders (Cesca 2012). Frankly, it appeared that the GOP's agenda was solely focused on ensuring that President Obama was not reelected. Republican Senate Minority Leader Mitch McConnell made a startling admission during President Obama's first term of office: "The single most important thing we [Republicans] want to achieve is for President Obama to be a one-term president" (Cesca 2012). Republicans failed in their efforts, and I am still wondering where the economy, gun control, unemployment, illegal immigration, and other important issues ranked on the GOP's to-do list.

To punctuate the racist environment President Obama endured throughout his first term: after Republican Colin Powell endorsed President Obama for reelection, Romney campaign surrogate John Sununu suggested that Powell's endorsement was motivated by race since both were African Americans. Powell made it crystal clear that his reasons for endorsing President Obama were not about race, but revolved around concerns with Romney's flip-flopping on various issues (Finocchiaro 2012). Powell's former Chief of Staff, Lawrence Wilkerson, also responded to Sununu's assertion with an angry rebuke:

> My party [the GOP] is full of racists, and the real reason a considerable portion of my party wants President Obama out of the White House has nothing to do with the content of his character, nothing to do with his competence as commander-in-chief and president, and everything to do with the color of his skin, and that's despicable. (Finocchiaro 2012)

President Obama's final story has yet to be written, especially regarding racism; however, conservative radio talk show host Rush

Limbaugh may have provided a subtle indication of things to come. On May 28, 2013, while discussing the relationship between President Obama and New Jersey Governor Chris Christie, Limbaugh described their relationship as a "master-servant relationship" with President Obama as the master with the money and Governor Christie as the servant who needed the money for Hurricane Sandy recovery aid (Gentilviso 2013). As innocuous as this description may seem and regardless of the fact that, in this case, the master was black and the servant was white; the use of the phrase "master-servant," could trigger thoughts of the "master-slave" relationship. I would be very surprised if Limbaugh was not aware of this as he was speaking.

On the website Salon.com, Joan Walsh made an interesting observation while discussing the October 2013 federal government shutdown and racist reactions to President Obama:

> Today [October 1, 2013], the entire government has been taken hostage by leaders elected by this crazed minority [Tea Party], who see in the face of Barack Obama everything they've been taught to fear for 50 years. Start with miscegenation: He's not just black, he's the product of a black father and a white mother … With his Ivy League degrees, they are sure he must be the elitist beneficiary of affirmative action. Steeped in Chicago politics, he's the representative of corrupt urban machines controlled by Democrats—machines that ironically originated with the Irish and once kept African Americans down, but which are now synonymous with corrupt black power. (Walsh 2013)

On a final note, in 2010, the website Examiner.com also pulled no punches regarding racist reactions to President Obama—comments that are still relevant in 2013:

> At a time when our country teetered on disaster thanks to the failed policies of [the] Bush administration and the thugs of Wall Street, one would think that the people of this nation across the racial spectrum would rally behind its President and Commander-in-Chief as every effort is being made to get the country back on track . . . But in lieu of a pat on the back,

this President [Obama] takes shots to the back. (Examiner.com 2010)

Why no pat on the back? President Obama is black. Then how did he get elected in the first place and reelected for a second term of office? An observation by Ta-Nehisi Coates in *The Atlantic* magazine provides an insightful answer: "Barack Obama governs a nation enlightened enough to send an African American to the White House, but not enlightened enough to accept a black man as its president" (Coates 2012).

—Clarence Thomas

In 1991, while serving as a US Court of Appeals judge, African American Clarence Thomas was accused of sexual harassment during his US Senate confirmation hearing to become a US Supreme Court associate justice. His accuser, Anita Hill, was an African American woman who was Thomas's assistant when he was with the US Department of Education and Chairman of the US Equal Employment Opportunity Commission. After credible testimony by Hill, the Senate still confirmed Thomas. As the news media seems to ignore black-on-black crime, did the Senate dismiss Hill's accusations in the same manner? I wonder whether Thomas would have been confirmed if Anita Hill were white.

Thomas's Senate confirmation hearing was an eye-opening experience, but not the source of my greatest concern. In my opinion, Justice Thomas is a dangerous racist ideologue. To be considered a racist rather than an annoying bigot, an individual must have the power to socioeconomically or politically impose his or her bigotry on others. As a member of the highest judicial authority in America, Justice Thomas is a bigot with enormous power that impacts all Americans, thus earning the title of racist. What is fueling his racist inclinations? Is it African Americans as a group, or the dark color of his own skin? If either one or both, Thomas is a "poster child" for and victim of the crippling effects of racism.

I heard an unconfirmed story that a Ku Klux Klan Grand Wizard once stated that violence against blacks was no longer part of the KKK modus operandi because of the increasing level of black-on-black crime. In other words, all the KKK had to do was sit back while blacks killed each other. If this was a true story, I would have to agree when analyzing

Justice Thomas. In my opinion, Thomas is "lynching" African Americans via retrograde and revisionist judicial opinions regarding civil rights in general, and specifically, affirmative action and similar civil rights gains—judicial black-on-black crime. Excerpts from a 2011 *New York Times* book review clearly make this point:

> It is incontestable that he [Thomas] has benefited from affirmative action at critical moments in his life, yet he denounces the policy and has persuaded himself that it played little part in his success. He berates disadvantaged people who view themselves as victims of racism and preaches an austere individualism, yet harbors self-pitying feelings of resentment and anger at his own experiences of racism . . . He is said to dislike light-skinned blacks, yet he is the legal guardian of a biracial child. (Patterson 2007)

While he consistently lambasts African Americans whom he feels are using racism as an excuse for being disenfranchised or victimized, it is ironic that Thomas played the victim when he "pulled the race card" in reaction to what he perceived as racist treatment during his Senate confirmation hearing. Thomas lamented:

> It's a national disgrace. And from my standpoint as a black American, as far as I'm concerned, it is a high-tech lynching for uppity blacks who in any way deign to think for themselves, to do for themselves, to have different ideas, and it is a message that unless you kowtow to an old order, this is what will happen to you. You will be lynched, destroyed, caricatured by a committee of the US Senate rather than hung from a tree. (Electronic Text Center)

As far as I am concerned, his comments were a blatant contradiction of his views regarding the use of racism as an excuse. *Is Justice Thomas a victim of racism when the mood suits him?*

Justice Thomas's life story has been a convoluted quagmire of poverty, racism, and acquired privilege. Again, this prompts questions about his comfort level accepting his own racial identity as a dark-skinned African American and, more importantly, his ability to render fair, well-reasoned, and judicially sound opinions on matters of race. Political analyst Earl Hutchison offered disturbing observations about Thomas, saying, "He has gone out of his way to thumb his nose at civil rights leaders and uphold some of the worst civil rights and civil liberties abuses even when that means on occasion breaking ranks with Scalia and casting the lone dissenting vote" (Hutchison 2011).

As one of many examples, Thomas rejects the idea that racial diversity has an educational benefit. He once wrote, "As should be obvious, there is nothing pressing or necessary about obtaining whatever educational benefits may flow from racial diversity" (Johnson 2013). Without further discussion, what happened to the educational benefits of learning from and exposure to the richness and experiences of racially diverse groups of people?

When Thomas was confirmed, A. Leon Higginbotham, Jr. was an African American US Court of Appeals judge who wrote a sixteen-page letter to Thomas. In the letter, Judge Higginbotham shared apprehensions regarding Thomas's dismissive views on race and civil rights, as well as his reluctance to respect the history, trials, and tribulations of African Americans who came before him and paved the way for Thomas's own success. Judge Higginbotham ended the letter with hopeful expectations:

> I trust you shall not forget that many who preceded you and many who follow you have found, and will find, the door of equal opportunity slammed in their faces through no fault of their own . . . I wish you well as a thoughtful and worthy successor to Justice Marshall in the ever ongoing struggle to assure equal justice under law for all persons. (A. Leon Higginbotham 1992)

Three years after Thomas's confirmation, Higginbotham reacted to Thomas's continued racist attitudes with a biting admonition during a 1994 lecture:

> I have often pondered how it is that Justice Thomas, an African American, could be so insensitive to the plight of the powerless. . . . I can only think of one Supreme Court justice during this century who was worse than Justice Clarence

Thomas—James McReynolds, a white supremacist who referred to blacks as niggers. (Fletcher 2007)

As a final observation, Justice Thomas remains silent on the bench; with one or two exceptions, over a twenty-year period, never asking questions or commenting during oral arguments. As the only African American US Supreme Court justice, his silence can give the impression he is dutifully deferring to his white colleagues.

Even though I have been very critical of Justice Thomas, I must give him credit for maintaining his convictions in the face of overwhelming criticism, especially from African Americans. With the exception of when he played the victim of racism during his confirmation hearing, Justice Thomas is consistent and, given his lifetime appointment, has no incentive to change. After all, a zebra does not change its stripes.

—Gabrielle "Gabby" Douglas

Colorism (a derivative of racism) showed its ugly face during the 2012 Summer Olympics. Dark-skinned African American gymnast Gabrielle "Gabby" Douglas was criticized for her "slicked-back" greasy hairstyle. This criticism was cruel, crass, and totally inappropriate, but it was even more disheartening that her critics were African American women who were probably indoctrinated to believe that long, greaseless, straight, or wavy hair was "good hair." "Good hair" is a catchphrase that describes white hairstyles that serve as a source of positive self-esteem and social stature among many African Americans.

Gabby's critics conveniently overlooked two facts. She styled her hair in such a manner to ensure it did not interfere with her performance, and there were no hairstylists available that were skilled in styling black hair.

Such criticism added credence to the stereotype that African Americans treat each other as "crabs in a barrel." A crab will pull down another crab that is climbing out of a barrel in an attempt to escape. In a social context, this catchphrase applies to an impoverished, disadvantaged, or disenfranchised group of people, such as African Americans, jealously trying to impede or denigrate the success of other members of the same group by pulling them back down to their level.

In support of Gabby, a woman named Jasmine Waiters wrote a very moving poem called "Ponytail." Please read or listen to it online, and all I will say to Gabby and others like her is, "You go girl!"

—Herman Cain

Herman Cain is a married African American who had to suspend his campaign to become the 2012 Republican presidential nominee due to sexual harassment allegations that surfaced *after* he became the front-runner. He was accused, by several white women, of sexual harassment that allegedly occurred when he was the head of the National Restaurant Association in the 1990s. Given his front-runner status in the Republican primaries, the timing of these allegations was exquisite.

On the other hand, Republican candidate Newt Gingrich had several extramarital affairs throughout the 1980s and 1990s. While Gingrich was Speaker of the US House of Representatives and leading an adulterous lifestyle, he hypocritically campaigned on family values, criticized others who were caught in similar behaviors, and led the failed attempt to impeach President Clinton when Clinton lied about his adulterous encounters. It was interesting that Gingrich's past marital indiscretions were mentioned during the 2012 primaries, but glossed over with little to no impact on his campaign. Gingrich is white and survived, yet Cain is black and had to withdraw. Form your own conclusions as to why.

—Paula Deen

Because of an admission during a 2013 legal deposition to using the n-word approximately thirty years ago, white celebrity chef and author Paula Deen was vilified in the court of public opinion even though she stated that she has not used such language since those days. Additionally, Deen's adult sons stated that they never heard her use a racial slur or convey a racist attitude. Nevertheless, she lost millions of dollars in corporate endorsements, the Food Network terminated her television contract, and her book publisher dropped her as a client. Were these reactions fair, or was Deen a scapegoat for past and present racism in America? Before attempting to answer this question, keep in mind that Deen was unsuccessfully sued for alleged discriminatory practices against employees and fostering a hostile work environment at her restaurant in Savanna, Georgia. The public storyline focused on her use of the n-word and not the lawsuit. This discussion will follow suit.

The use of the n-word was and still is an unfortunate part of America's vocabulary, especially in southern locales such as Deen's birthplace—Albany, Georgia. When I became a young adult and experienced the harsh realities of racism, I reacted by using racial slurs to pejoratively describe white people. I also used the n-word while jokingly or affectionately referring to African Americans. Many years ago, I evolved to the point where racial slurs were no longer in my vocabulary or part of my thinking process. Because I used racial slurs decades ago, would this make me worthy of scorn today?

From a Christian perspective, I am reminded of a biblical passage in the Holy Bible, when Jesus saved a woman from being stoned to death for committing adultery: "And Jesus said unto her, Neither do I condemn thee: go, and sin no more" (John 8:11, King James Version).

Simply put, a person may have done something wrong in the past, but if corrective and redemptive action is taken, there should be no further condemnation. Assuming Paula Deen and her sons are telling the truth, should she be treated any differently than Jesus treated the biblical adulteress? For me or anyone else who has used racial slurs in the past, but appropriately evolved, to treat Deen with derision for doing exactly what we did would be the epitome of hypocrisy.

To garner votes for the 1964 Civil Rights Act, President Lyndon Johnson used the n-word while privately pandering to southern members of Congress to garner support for the Civil Rights Act. Was President Johnson wrong? Yes. But was he scorned *after* the Civil Rights Act was signed into law and his n-word usage became public knowledge? Alabama Governor George Wallace was a staunch segregationist until he was shot and had an epiphany resulting in a cathartic apology for past racist behaviors. He became a committed advocate for black constituents during and after his final term of office. Was he wrong and vilified for past racist behaviors? Yes. But was he scorned *after* his transformation?

The Framers of the US Constitution are viewed with reverence even though many owned slaves—a practice obviously far worse than uttering racial slurs. However, their ownership of slaves is historically minimized because of their roles in the writing of the Constitution. Even though Paula Deen does not share the same celebrity as President Johnson, Governor Wallace, or the Framers, for the sake of consistent and equitable treatment, should she not be given the same consideration for prior bad acts—equal justice for all?

Given this background, if Deen's current racial inclinations and behaviors are not reflective of past behaviors, the retribution directed at her is hypocritical and forgiveness must prevail. If retribution is the new standard of punishment for prior bad acts that have since been rehabilitated, America would be overwhelmed with black and white Americans eligible for similar retribution—myself included. Americans must remember that when you point one finger, there are three fingers pointing back at you.

—Rachel Jeantel

During the 2013 murder trial of George Zimmerman, Rachel Jeantel testified as a prosecution witness. Other than Zimmerman, Rachel was the last person to talk to Trayvon Martin before his death. When Rachel testified, there were immediate reactions to her demeanor and manner of speaking. In my opinion, she was racially stereotyped because she was a dark-skinned, plus-sized black girl from a low-income neighborhood, did not speak the King's English, and could not read cursive writing even though she was a nineteen-year-old high school senior.

Additionally, it seemed the defense and prosecuting attorneys were totally unaware of Rachel's life, environment, and social frame of reference, i.e., a nineteen-year-old of Haitian descent who knew nothing of the world other than her neighborhood and grew up speaking Spanish and Creole with English as a third language. The cultural divide between Rachel's views of the world as compared to mainstream America's expectations of behavior was gaping. This became glaringly apparent during the cross-examination. During the first day of her cross-examination by the defense, Rachel displayed irritability and frustration with the questioning. In response, white defense attorney Don West was aggressive with and, at times, condescending toward Rachel. On the second day of her cross-examination, when Rachel appeared calmer and addressed him as "Sir," West asked Rachel, "You feeling okay today? You seem different than yesterday" (Schneider and Hightower 2013). In a trial permeated with racial overtones, West's question and observation could be perceived as a patronizing, master-slave "now that's a good nigger" response versus a race-neutral conciliatory inquiry.

To the best of my knowledge, there is no direct correlation between a person's appearance, demeanor, or manner of speaking and the truthfulness of a person's comments; however, in Rachel's case, a direct correlation was apparently made. Because many saw Rachel as uneducated, with a "thuggish" and defiant attitude, her testimony was viewed as not credible, thus reinforcing racial stereotypes of black teens that many Americans still embrace. These stereotypes were perpetuated in judgmental news coverage, disparaging social network communications, and by white female Juror B37 who stated that Rachel's testimony was not credible. For example, on Twitter, Rachel was compared to Aunt Jemima and Precious (a troubled dark-skinned and obese African American teenager in the 2009 movie *Precious*). Juror B37 was interviewed by CNN's Anderson Cooper and made the following stereotypical and patronizing statement: "I think she [Rachel] felt inadequate toward everyone because of her education and her communication skills. I just felt sadness for her" (Serwer 2013).

I found this curious when comparing the treatment of Rachel with that of a light-skinned Asian prosecution witness, Associate Medical Examiner Dr. Shiping Bao. Dr. Bao's testimony was fraught with flip-flopping opinions and, similar to Rachel, difficulties speaking the King's English, and at times, defiance and defensiveness. Contrary to Rachel's treatment, Dr. Bao's Asian ethnicity and racial stereotypes were not mentioned in the criticism he received regarding the quality of his testimony. If Rachel was light-skinned, had "good hair," and was articulate while testifying, I believe evaluations of her testimony would have focused on the content of her testimony and not her appearance, demeanor, or ethnicity—a perfect segue to a discussion about colorism.

Colorism

In the movie *Red Tails*, a white bomber pilot asks a group of black fighter pilots what "colored" pilots preferred to be called. A black pilot replied with the observation, "When you run out of air, you turn blue. When you grow envious, you turn green. When you're afraid, you turn yellow—and then you call *us* 'colored'?" (Vyan 2012). In other words, skin color should not be part of the discussion, but racism and colorism dictate otherwise.

Colorism is a quaint word that describes applications of discriminatory practices based on the light or dark skin complexion of African Americans. Colorism has a global reach, especially in countries with a significant black population; however, I will focus on colorism in America. Again, it is politely called colorism, but regardless of what it is called, colorism is just another aspect of racism.

Please reflect on the answer given by a dark-skinned African American child during the 2011 TV documentary *Dark Girls* when asked how she felt about being called black:

Child: "I don't like to be called black."
Interviewer: "Why?"
Child: "Because I'm not black."
(Duke and Berry 2011)

Colorism has several facets. It mirrors the ongoing practice of white supremacy in that African Americans with lighter skin receive privileges not given to darker-skinned peers (Nittle). As stated earlier, Paula Deen was unsuccessfully sued for alleged discriminatory practices against her employees. One of the allegations was she preferred whites and light-skinned blacks to work with customers, and darker-skinned blacks were relegated to unseen "back-of-the-house" operations (Jeffries and Washington 2013).

Is it a coincidence that since the latter part of the twentieth century, most African Americans who reached the executive or similar levels of power in business or government are light-skinned, with most having "good hair"? For example, Colin Powell, America's first African American chairman of the Joint Chiefs of Staff, national security advisor, and secretary of state, is light-skinned, as are President Obama, US Attorney General Eric Holder, and UN Ambassador Susan Rice. The first African American US Supreme Court justice, Thurgood Marshall, was also light-skinned. Michelle Obama, Herman Cain, Oprah Winfrey, Condoleezza Rice, and Clarence Thomas are notable darker-skinned exceptions; however, all the women maintain "good hair."

Colorism can also be discussed in the context of hostility between light- and dark-skinned African Americans in general, and specifically between African Americans who look, act, and sound black and those who do not. Below are several derogatory terms African Americans hurl at each other, with most directed at African Americans who do not look, sound, or act black:

- "High yellow" or "redbone": Very light-skinned, or suggesting mixed parentage.
- "Bougie," "uppity," or "sadiddy": Having an elitist attitude.

- "Oreo": Looks black on the outside, but acts white.
- "Uncle Tom": Overly subservient to whites.

Let's examine the origins of this hostility. During slavery, class distinctions were clearly delineated by elitist and privileged slaves who worked in the slave master's home as compared to the less privileged who toiled in the fields—setting the stage for colorism's emergence. During the postslavery Jim Crow era, colorism manifested itself through racist scenarios such as the notorious Paper Bag Test. African Americans with a skin color lighter than a paper lunch bag ("house slaves") were allowed entry into black fraternities, sororities, and other bastions of the black elite, while darker-skinned peers ("field slaves") were excluded. Along with the Paper Bag Test, there were the Comb and Pencil tests that measured the coarseness of the hair to ensure it was "good hair," as well as the Flashlight Test that examined a black person's profile to ensure facial features were similar to those of the white race ("Discrimination based on skin color").

These tests and related elitist attitudes planted the seeds of racial animosity between light- and dark-skinned African Americans and resulted in future generations of African Americans—especially children—measuring their self-esteem and social worth by using skin complexion and hair texture as defining standards, i.e., the lighter and straighter, the better. Reflecting on the mind-set behind these tests and standards, I found it curious that Benjamin Jealous, the current CEO of the bedrock of black civil rights organizations, the NAACP, is a very light-skinned biracial African American with "good hair" who, in my opinion, could easily pass as white—prototypical colorism?

For black women, colorism further manifests itself through the Lena Horne Syndrome. This syndrome described African American women who bleached their skin to lighten their skin color and straightened their hair in order to pass as white, appear more socially acceptable in a white-dominated society, or artificially bolster individual self-esteem and sense of beauty. Black-oriented magazines colluded with this syndrome by advertising skin-lightening and hair-straightening products, products that have grown into a global multi-billion-dollar industry. In regard to hair, black males acquired "good hair" through hairstyles such as conks and pompadours (artificially straightened, wavy, or slicked-back hair)

protected by Do-Rags (scarfs worn to maintain these hairstyles)—
hairstyles that are now, for the most part, extinct.

Using female fashion models as a benchmark, the fashion website
Fashionista presented an interesting perspective on measures of beauty.
According to the most recent census, 36 percent of Americans now
identify as non-Caucasian as compared to 16 percent in 1970. For
decades, the standard of beauty was white with blond hair, blue eyes,
and Nordic features. However, as described by model casting director
Julia Samersova, even though the modeling industry is still dominated
by white models, it is acknowledging the increasing numbers of
non-Caucasians in America and slowly evolving to a more diverse
standard of beauty: "The All American look today is what America
looks like in general . . . We are the melting pot of the world! Black,
Hispanic, Native American, Asian, and Caucasian. That is the beauty of
the All American look—we can *blend* all these gorgeous races together!"
(Fashionista).

On the surface, this evolution to "blended" physical features
and lightly hued skin colors can be viewed as a victory for diversity;
however, this is also a victory for colorism. The evolving standards of
beauty are still based on "good hair," light skin, and "less black" physical
features—standards even children understand.

During the 1940s, husband and wife psychologists Kenneth and
Mamie Clark designed a test, commonly known as the Doll Test, to
study the psychological effects of racism on black children. In exercises
requiring black children to evaluate the skin color of various dolls, the
children had an overwhelming tendency to pick light-colored or white
dolls as the "preferred" or "good" dolls. During a drawing exercise, the
following results mirrored previous test results:

> The Clarks also gave the children outline drawings of a boy
> and girl and asked them to color the figures the same color
> as themselves. Many of the children with dark complexions
> colored the figures with a white or yellow crayon. The Clarks
> concluded that "prejudice, discrimination, and segregation"
> caused black children to develop a sense of inferiority and
> self-hatred. (Library of Congress)

Over time, variations of the test have been conducted, and the results were strikingly consistent with the original results. The interviewed African American child's discomfort with being called black and denial of her ethnicity becomes easier to understand.

With this background, please consider colorism's impact on my family. One of my grandmothers was the daughter of the white son of a former slave owner and a black woman he allegedly raped in segregationist Georgia. Even though her siblings were allowed to leave home, my grandmother was kept at home because she was very light-skinned and attractive, with "good hair." Because of her fair complexion and beauty, my great-grandfather had concerns that if she went away to college, she would not return home or may be raped if she ventured far from home. In short, my grandmother was treated not as an emancipated black woman, but as a light-skinned trophy of color—white-on-black colorism.

My mother was raised by light-skinned black parents in the white, middle-class section of a New Jersey town. She was also very light-skinned and attractive, with "good hair," and always avoided the use of idioms, manner of speaking, and social behaviors commonly associated with blacks. She graduated with honors from Wilberforce University and was a lifetime member of the Delta Sigma Theta sorority—both institutions of the black elite at that time. As the wife of a black US Army officer, my mother had to interact with a black military community that did not relate to or accept her demeanor. She was labeled as being "uppity" and subsequently ostracized—black-on-black colorism. In order to be accepted by her peers, my mother had to make difficult adjustments to how she interacted with other African Americans, an experience I would also endure.

As I grew up as a light-skinned African American during the Civil Rights era, colorism had a crushing impact on my maturation. I never heard of Ebonics and sounded white. I was raised on overseas and domestic military bases, and in middle-class white neighborhoods that conditioned me to the ways of the "white world" at the expense of not having a black experience or understanding the nuances of being black. Throughout my upbringing, I attended majority-white schools and, with one exception, all my childhood friends were white. This exposed a brutal truth that would later have painful consequences. I was black, but did not know anything about being black—I was a "high-yellow Oreo" who had to deal with confusing racial contradictions that had crippling effects on my self-image as I matured into adulthood.

This conflict climaxed when I left home to attend West Point. Even though I sounded and acted white, I looked black and had to endure racist reactions from various white classmates and upperclassmen, especially during my Plebe (freshman) year. Because I did not sound or act black, I was belittled by black classmates until, as occurred with my mother, I made chameleon-like adjustments such that my persona was more aligned with the stereotypical black norms of behavior and manner of speaking—black-on-black colorism.

I did not experience a crisis regarding my racial identity because my physical features and both of my parents were black. Again, my conflict was associated with self-image. As a light-skinned African American with a white-oriented upbringing, I did not know where I belonged in black or white America—one of the most debilitating effects of colorism. As I had to learn how to navigate through a clearly defined world of black or white, a growing number of today's youth have a similar, but more complicated road to travel—the consequences of being biracial or multiracial with melting-pot or white-looking physical features that cannot be easily characterized as belonging to one race or another.

As occurred with me, the confusing impacts of colorism become immediately apparent through the emergence of self-image crises among these children. This confusion is exacerbated when physical features and mixed parentage are such that one does not neatly fit into a particular ethnic category. It is no longer a simple choice of black or white, as it was for me. It is now many shades of ethnic grey, as demonstrated when light-skinned multiracial golfer Tiger Woods refused to describe himself as an African American and was subsequently criticized, especially by African Americans. His late father was African American with Chinese and Native American ancestry, and his mother is Thai with Dutch and Chinese ancestry. To address all the components of his family lineage, Woods defiantly created the unique descriptor "Cablinasian" (**Ca**ucasian, **Bl**ack, American **In**dian, and **Asian**) to ethnically identify himself (Urban Dictionary).

In a society conditioned to place Americans into neat ethnic boxes such as Black, White, Native American, Hispanic, or Asian, what does a biracial or multiracial American select when officially asked for his or her race? The perfect example of this conundrum was the 2010 US

Census form. If a person was biracial or multiracial, he or she had to check "Some other race" and then handwrite an answer (Humes, Jones, and Ramirez 2011).

Contemporary colorism also prompts interesting life decisions, as evidenced during the 2012 CNN documentary *Who is Black in America.* A biracial teenage girl who looks white, but considers herself an African American, identifies herself as "White/Caucasian" on college and job applications in order to avoid racial discrimination. During an exercise, another light-skinned biracial teenage girl who looks black, but is reluctant to identify herself as an African American, is asked to choose a chair that best describes her. Each chair has a placard with one personal descriptor written on it, such as white, black, or Native American. She chooses a chair with a placard that reads "Female." Prior to this exercise, in an attempt to avoid having to make an ethic choice, she classified herself as "human" in a poem she had written. However, in America, because she looks black, she will always be seen and treated as a black person. Finally coming to this realization, she eventually identifies herself as an African American (CNN and Soledad O'Brien 2012). Both teenagers present thought-provoking and emotional solutions to a complicated problem and prompt a question. Given the growing number of biracial and multiracial Americans, will African Americans eventually disappear as an ethnic group and be replaced by a hybrid light-skinned race yet to be named—colorism's end game?

As a closing thought, reacting to people that look, act, or sound different will always be a component of human nature; however, how we react is critical. Do we embrace hurtful "isms," such as colorism, or do we leverage the richness of our differences? While addressing humanity's place in the world, Dr. Jill Bolte Taylor posed a similar question: "How do we each, as individuals of a collective whole called humanity, bring our gifts to the table to be a part of the solution?" (Taylor 2013).

Better yet, how do we each, as individuals of a collective called Americans who are much more than the color or complexion of our skin, bring our gifts and not our bigotry to the table to be a part of the solution? Hopefully, America will eventually find an answer that results in the demise of colorism because, as stated by India.Arie in her song "I Am Not My Hair":

I am not my hair.
I am not this skin.
I am a soul that lives within.
(India.Arie 2006)

New N-Words

Before starting this discussion, explaining the origin of the n-word will be necessary to provide background and context.

Nigger, or the truncated versions *nigga* or *niggra,* is a racial slur referring to African Americans or anyone who looks black. *Nigger* originated as a neutral term referring to black people, a variation of the Spanish/Portuguese noun *negro* that is a descendant of the Latin word *niger.* In antebellum Southern states, *nigger* was used as a benign racial descriptor specifically referring to slaves and free blacks. After the Civil War, *nigger* morphed into a maliciously pejorative racial slur that continues to plague African Americans today ("Nigger"). Since *nigger* is such an odious slur, the "n-word" was created as a socially palatable substitution and politically correct euphemism.

Unfortunately and in my opinion, *nigger* and its accompanying mentality have been figuratively applied to two new groups of people in America—illegal immigrants and Muslims.

—(Illegal) Immigrant

Illegal immigration has become such a hot-button issue in southwestern states, such as Arizona, that (illegal) immigrant is now an n-word in those states and is slowly becoming one throughout America.

To understand the scope of illegal immigration into America, note the origin of illegal immigrants by global region in 2009. Ninety-one percent came from global regions predominantly populated by people of color, or more specifically, the Caribbean (4 percent), Mexico (59 percent), Central and South America combined (17 percent), and Asia (11 percent)—statistics that are probably accurate in 2013 (Germano 2011). Additionally, in fiscal year 2012, America spent more money (nearly $18 billion) on immigration enforcement than all other federal law enforcement agencies combined (Foley 2013).

America's immigration policies are in need of comprehensive reform, especially in the area of leveraging highly skilled immigrants who are legally in America with work or student visas. However, the illegal immigration debate has overshadowed issues concerning legal immigrants. Consequently, this discussion will concentrate on illegal immigration.

As background, consider this famous proclamation from the poem *The New Colossus*, written by American poet Emma Lazarus in 1883:

> Give me your tired, your poor,
> Your huddled masses yearning to breathe free,
> The wretched refuse of your teeming shore.
> Send these, the homeless, tempest-tost [sic] to me,
> I lift my lamp beside the golden door!

This proclamation refers to immigration and is inscribed on a plaque in the museum located under the Statue of Liberty. However, the lamp is extinguished, and the golden door is closed to all illegal immigrants.

I hope most Americans believe as I do, that immigrants need to enter America legally. But I have to pragmatically take into account the millions of illegal immigrants already in America—one reason for an amnesty program. An overwhelming majority of illegal immigrants come to America to seek honest work and acquire a better standard of living for themselves or their families—another reason for amnesty. As an aside, why can't amnesty be offered to illegal immigrants? After all, President Nixon was pardoned for high crimes associated with the Watergate scandal, and the convictions or sentences of criminals can be commuted, or they can receive pardons or parole. Also, if Cubans can be offered a path to permanent US residency if they reach American soil under the Wet Foot Dry Foot policy, why can't the same consideration be given to illegal immigrants already on American soil?

Usually paid below minimum wage, illegal immigrants are often hired as domestic workers, trusted to clean our homes and look after our children. *Are illegal immigrants only considered valuable assets when the mood suits us and no one is looking?* Dolores Huerta, cofounder of the United Farm Workers, stated:

We learn to look down on people who grow our food, make our clothes, build our roads. We blame immigrants for our economic problems, while they work under dangerous conditions for substandard wages. NOW [National Organization of Women] recognizes that racism, sexism, and classism all work together. (Huerta)

When illegal immigrants are captured, they are detained, may appear in a US Administrative Court, and are usually deported. Some exceptions to deportation are immigrants who apply for political asylum and Cubans who reach American soil under the Wet Foot Dry Foot policy. Also, illegal immigrants convicted of a crime must serve their sentences before deportation. This seems appropriate, but what about American business owners and homeowners who enable illegal immigration by hiring undocumented workers? If American businesses and homeowners refused to hire undocumented workers, the influx of illegal immigrants would decrease dramatically. There are penalties for hiring undocumented workers; however, in my opinion, they are not enforced enough. It is one thing to prosecute a weaker and lesser-advantaged group such as illegal immigrants, but apparently it is another matter to prosecute affluent and mostly white home and business owners.

In 2012, illegal immigration from Mexico decreased to the slowest rate since 1971. Two possible reasons for the decrease were the increase in deportations during the Obama administration and significant loss of income and job opportunities due to America's postrecession economy. The Pew Hispanic Center reported that the influx of illegal immigrants from Mexico may have even reversed itself (Spagat 2012). Having said this, amnesty for illegal immigrants is still a polarizing issue in America.

Many conservatives oppose an amnesty program; however, a bipartisan group of US senators sponsored immigration reform legislation that was passed by the US Senate and sent to the House of Representatives in June 2013. This legislation would give illegal immigrants provisional legal status and the ability to legally obtain employment, an opportunity to apply for permanent residency, and a path to eventual citizenship, but getting legislation through the GOP-controlled House of Representatives and to the president's desk will be a very arduous journey.

With this background, how can America finally resolve the illegal immigration problem? I propose a four-step approach, components of which may or may not be included in the US Senate legislation:

1. Do not let partisan politics derail the process due to petty bickering over the name of the program. Calling this an amnesty, probation, or facetiously an "all-y all-y in come free" (children's game proclamation to tell undiscovered players to show themselves without a game penalty) program is not germane to what needs to be done. The content of the legislation would be the law of the land—not the name of the legislation.

2. For illegal immigrants already in America, create a one-time-only amnesty program with these components:

   o Extend the Cuban Wet Foot Dry Foot policy to all in-country illegal immigrants as part of an amnesty program. Subject to clean background checks, illegal immigrants on American soil can stay in a multiyear probationary status, apply for green cards or work permits, and eventually follow a path to permanent residency and ultimately citizenship (US Immigration Support).

   o Register all illegal immigrants for identification and tracking purposes. The existing E-Verify system could be used, or we could look at India's unique identification project where a twelve-digit unique number will be issued to all residents in India. The number would be stored in a centralized database and linked to basic demographics and biometric information (photograph, fingerprints, DNA, and eyes) of each individual. It is easily verifiable in an online and cost-effective manner, and also unique enough to eliminate the possibility of duplicate and fake identities ("Unique Identification Authority of India").

   o Within an appropriate period of time, require amnesty program participants to pay applicable back taxes and a one-time penalty for illegally entering America, learn English, and pass a test to ensure basic understanding of America's government functions, the US Constitution, and applicable laws. Failure to complete any step would result in the loss of probationary status, removal from the amnesty program, and deportation.

o Effective the first day of the amnesty program, criminalize illegal immigration by making it a federal crime subject to a one-year prison sentence for first-time offenders and more severe sentences for repeat offenders. Illegally entering America is tantamount to criminal trespass and should be treated accordingly. Currently, it is only a violation of US administrative law, which is why, with some exceptions, deportation is the only consequence—a consequence not compelling enough to prevent a deported immigrant from trying again.

o All apprehended illegal minors should be placed in the custody of child protective services as a ward of the state and reunited with their parents when the parents have served their sentences and are deported back to their country of origin. If a child turns eighteen before his or her parents have completed their sentences, the child should be considered an adult and deported back to his or her country of origin. Hopefully, the threat of prison incarceration and family separation will deter family units from illegally entering America.

o Effective the first day of the amnesty program, sanction a captured illegal immigrant's country of origin for the cost of apprehension, prosecution, incarceration, and subsequent deportation.

o Deny amnesty to all who have been convicted of a felony in America or any other country.

o From the first day of the program, in-country illegal immigrants would have one year to register with the Immigration and Naturalization Service. Also extend amnesty to American businesses and homeowners for one year so they can declare all undocumented workers in their employment.

3. Concurrent with the start of the amnesty program:
   o Secure America's borders with special attention to the *entire* Mexico/US border. A border wall has already been built along portions of the border. A wall invokes memories of

the infamous Cold War Berlin Wall in Germany, but if this is the only solution to stem the flow of illegal immigrants from Mexico, extend the wall to cover the entire border.
o   Increase federal funding to bolster staffing, infrastructure, and surveillance technologies to cover the entire Mexico/US border.

4. At the end of the amnesty program, impose additional provisions and penalties:
    o   If illegal immigration is criminalized under the RICO statute, prosecute business owners and homeowners who *knowingly* employ or harbor illegal immigrants. Knowingly employing illegal immigrants could be legally construed as an act in furtherance of a criminal conspiracy or enterprise.
    o   Continue the ethical practice of treating all illegal immigrants in need of medical care, but require medical facilities to report to US Immigration and Customs Enforcement (ICE) or appropriate immigration service all patients without valid identification, such as a social security or state identification card, driver's license, green card, or valid US or foreign passport with a current visa. It would be ICE's, not the medical facility's, responsibility to follow up. This recommendation should be enacted *only if illegal immigration is criminalized.* Medical facilities are currently required to report gunshot wounds and other suspicious injuries, such as suspected child abuse, to the local police. Also, if stopped by the police for a traffic violation, the driver is usually required to produce a valid license and proof of insurance. If the driver cannot produce either of these documents, he or she could be ticketed or arrested. Going to a medical facility without valid identification should be treated no differently; however, *if illegal immigration is not criminalized,* medical care should be provided under current reporting protocols.

Ironically, most Americans objecting to an amnesty program are descendants of immigrants. There is credible evidence to accuse many of these ancestral immigrants of illegally migrating into America's western frontier, where they forcibly evicted Native Americans from their tribal homelands and continually violated federal treaties. Additionally, white immigrants and their descendants perpetuated slavery and the exploitation of Asian immigrants, with slaves and Asian immigrants performing the same menial labor most illegal immigrants perform today. Americans objecting to amnesty should consider that many of their ancestors basically received amnesty for slavery and the exploitation of other people of color. Also, America's history would have been dramatically altered if Native Americans had killed or forcibly evicted the original Mayflower pilgrims versus offering sanctuary and forming symbiotic relationships—an altruistic lesson Americans need to remember while considering amnesty for present-day illegal immigrants.

Federal immigration legislation, the Dream Act, would have provided illegal immigrants permanent residency if they showed good moral character, attended college, or enlisted in the military, but it was voted down in 2010. In 2012, President Obama issued an executive order for illegal immigrants brought to America as children. This executive order established the Deferred Action for Childhood Arrivals program, wherein qualifying illegal immigrants can defer and eventually avoid deportation if they meet certain criteria (Cohen 2012). Regardless of stop-gap remedies, until a comprehensive and permanent solution is found to legally integrate illegal immigrants into American society, they will continue to be regarded as an n-word and prompt questions as to whether America is truly the land of the free.

As a closing note and message to Congress, 2,228 illegal immigrants were released from federal detention in February 2013 (Caldwell 2013). If the federal government is comfortable with reintroducing detained illegal immigrants back into American society, albeit supervised and still subject to deportation, America should be comfortable with giving qualified illegal immigrants amnesty along with a path to permanent residency and, ultimately, citizenship. Hopefully, by the time *We the Who?* is published, immigration reform will be a reality, thus removing the n-word mantle from these immigrants.

—Muslim

On September 11, 2001, the World Trade Center was destroyed by Islamic al-Qaeda terrorists who were of Middle Eastern descent (people of color); resulting in "Muslim" becoming another n-word. After 9/11,

Muslims and others of Middle Eastern descent became instant pariahs in America, reigniting religious and racial hostilities dating back to the Holy Crusades. After 9/11, a Sikh was mistaken for a Muslim and killed because he wore a turban. After the 2013 Boston Marathon bombing, a Muslim woman wearing a hijab was assaulted by a white male who shouted that Muslims were responsible for the bombing.

However, Timothy McVeigh, the Oklahoma City bomber who killed 168 men, women, and children, was white, a Republican, and Catholic. Did Americans vilify or attack whites, Republicans, and Catholics? As occurred with the proposed construction of Islamic mosques after 9/11, did Americans protest the construction of Catholic churches in their neighborhoods? With this background and by way of comparison, let's look at similar, but hypothetical, scenarios.

If the 9/11 attackers were white Protestant militia members, I believe all whites and Protestants would escape retribution. If the attackers were white Muslim Americans, I believe whites would escape retribution, but Muslims would still be vilified even though they were white. If the attackers were African American Christians, Christians would escape retribution, but I believe African Americans would have to run for their lives. As far as I am concerned, race and religion play a dominate role in determining how Americans react.

There are historical precedents for my conclusions; America's history of racial and religious intolerance is self-evident. America treated Japanese Americans as n-words and detained them in internment camps during WWII. Were white German Americans and Italian Americans detained in internment camps? Again, let's not forget how America treated Native Americans, as n-words, when they were forcibly evicted from their tribal homelands and relocated to federal reservations that exist to this day. Now consider the indefinite detention of suspected or confirmed Muslim terrorists without a trial or due process of law at the Guantanamo Bay Detention Center, a subject to be further discussed in chapter 2, "Justice."

Is the root of the deep-seated rancor against Muslims about religion or racial differences? Both play a part, which is why many Muslim Americans (especially of color) are currently viewed with derision and suspicion—as n-words—by many Americans. Many Christian Americans may not realize that Islam parallels Christianity in many areas. For example, the Christian archangel Gabriel, who told the Virgin Mary that she would give birth to Jesus, is mentioned in the Quran with the Arabic name of Jibrail. Jibrail is the greatest of the angels in Islam and revealed the Quran to the Prophet Muhammad. In Islam, Jesus is considered to be a messenger of God, and his virgin birth is discussed in the Quran. With these similarities, it is a shame that the messages of peace and respect contained in the Holy Bible and Quran are not practiced by misguided, racist, or extremist Judeo-Christians such as Timothy McVeigh and Muslim terrorists.

During a congressional hearing investigating the alleged radicalization of Islam, US Representative Keith Ellison (an African American Muslim) spoke about a New York City Police Department cadet and paramedic named Mohammed Salman Hamdani. Hamdani, a Pakistani-born Muslim American, died while attempting to save people from the World Trade Center on 9/11. These were Ellison's poignant comments:

> Mr. Hamdani bravely sacrificed his life to try to help others on 9/11. After the tragedy some people tried to smear his character solely because of his Islamic faith. Some people spread false rumors, and speculated that he was involved with the attackers because he was a Muslim. But it was only when his remains were identified that these lies were exposed. Mohammed Salman Hamdani was a fellow American who gave his life for other Americans. *His life should not be just a member of an ethnic group or just a member of a religion, but as an American who gave everything for his fellow Americans.* (Fabian 2011, italics mine)

In contrast, a Muslim man named Usman Farman fell down with a debris cloud, from a collapsing World Trade Center tower, fast approaching. A fleeing Hasidic Jew stopped and extended a helping hand while imploring Farman to get up: "Brother, if you don't mind, there is a cloud of glass coming at us, grab my hand, let's get the hell out of here" (Botelho 2002). They both escaped unharmed—so much for racial bigotry, religious intolerance, and the n-word mentality.

Sandy Hook and Chicago: A Tale of Two Cities

Since the advent of televised news, it has been the norm for white-on-white and black-on-white crime to get extensive news coverage and national attention while most black-on-black and brown-on-brown (Hispanic) crime receives rudimentary attention. For example, let's examine the news coverage and reactions associated with the 2012 Sandy Hook Elementary School shooting as compared to the announcement of Chicago's five hundredth homicide in 2012—a tale of two cities with racial undercurrents.

Sandy Hook is a majority-white affluent village in the town of Newtown, Connecticut. On December 14, 2012, an emotionally disturbed white male shot and killed twenty white first-grade school children (one of whom may have been biracial), six white adult members of the Sandy Hook Elementary School staff, and his mother before he committed suicide. The response to the shooting was immediate and nationwide. News coverage was continuous, with news commentators setting up camp in Newtown. Sporting, social, and political events had moments of silence for the victims, gun-control debates exploded, and President Obama traveled to Newtown to deliver an address and subsequently ordered American flags to half-staff. The angry outcry continued for months—an understandable nationwide reaction.

On December 28, 2012, Chicago announced its 500th homicide for the year. There was a ripple of news coverage and hardly any national reaction before attention returned to Sandy Hook. This lack of attention was interesting, because data showed that African Americans and Hispanics represented 92 percent of the 500 homicides, with the youngest victim being three weeks old. The final total of Chicago homicides in 2012 was 515, of which 441 were gun fatalities. Seventy-nine percent, or 350 of the 441 gun fatality victims, were people of color, and 124 of the 441 gun fatalities were age twenty or younger (Swartz). Granted, not all the gun fatalities were children, yet where was the national outrage for the loss of life that far exceeded Sandy Hook? Throughout the year, news coverage about Chicago's homicide rate was short-lived and scant—obligatory television commentary, a few days of political and public outcry, and then back to business as usual (Guarino 2012).

Chicago and Sandy Hook elicited two very different responses to the same type of tragedy, multiple gun-related homicides that included children. According to the Children's Defense Fund, African American children accounted for 45 percent of the gun fatalities in America during 2009 and 2010 (World of NEWSNINJA2012 2012), yet how many people in America were aware of this, or worse, even cared?

In my opinion, one reason for the lack of attention to Chicago and other inner-city homicides is the reality that multiple murders of low-income children of color are not as newsworthy as multiple murders of white affluent children. Another reason is that most inner-city homicides and related gun violence are gang-related. "Gang-related" is code for black/brown-on-black/brown crime, which again rarely receives noteworthy national attention. Gang violence and related homicides among people of color are so prevalent and engrained in the American psyche that they do not garner the same visceral reactions as the murder of white children and are viewed by a desensitized America as the status quo of inner-city life. These reasons are brutally insensitive and blatantly racist.

The loss of twenty-seven innocent lives in Sandy Hook was tragic, but the loss of 515 lives in one year was far worse. Before the Sandy Hook shooting, Newtown only had one homicide in the past ten years, for a current total of twenty-eight homicides. In the same ten-year period, Chicago saw over 5,000 homicides, a high percentage of which were gun-related. For additional perspective, in 1991 alone, Chicago experienced 922 homicides, with 262 of these homicides being children (Recktenwald 1992). In accordance with the current trend, I am assuming that most were children of color. Also, 640 or 69 percent of the 922 homicides were gun-related (Chicago Police Department 2012). Even at these high homicide levels, there was hardly a mention from the news media, government, and public in general, and I have not included the homicide rates of other major cities, such as Los Angeles, St. Louis, Philadelphia, Detroit, and New York City.

Princeton University professor Dr. Cornel West made some interesting comments about gun-related violence. "Not a peep, not a mumbling word when black folk get shot," he said, "but now, Newtown, Connecticut, vanilla side—lo and behold, we got a major conversation. That's wonderful. Each life is precious, but it just upsets me when we're so deferential" (Rothman 2012).

After the Sandy Hook shooting, even white conservative radio talk show host Rush Limbaugh criticized the news media for their collective disinterest in urban gun violence (Rothman 2012). Dr. West called it "deferential." I call it racist, and President Obama reinforced the perception of racism by traveling to Newtown. His intentions were honorable and supportive, but he apparently forgot that perception can also be another person's reality. Let me explain.

Prior to the Sandy Hook shooting, where else had President Obama traveled in response to gun violence in America? To the best of my knowledge, nowhere. He finally visited Chicago *two months after* the Sandy Hook tragedy to deliver an address on gun violence and, prior to this trip, First Lady Michelle Obama attended the funeral service for Hadiya Pendleton—a fifteen-year-old African American drum majorette who participated in the 2013 presidential inaugural parade. Hadiya was shot and killed in Chicago eight days after the parade. If Hadiya did not have the newsworthy notability of participating in the inaugural parade and was just one of many inner-city homicides lost in the statistics, would the First Lady have attended the funeral? I doubt it. I believe neither she nor President Obama would have known or been told about the homicide. In addition to showing support and sympathy, I also wonder whether her trip had a secondary objective of making a political statement in support of President Obama's resurrected gun-control efforts. On an encouraging note, the First Lady attended a conference on youth violence and visited a Chicago high school hard hit by gun violence, and President Obama toured the country to garner support for gun-control legislation—better late than never.

I hope this heightened attention continues because, prior to the Sandy Hook shooting, President Obama had been reticent on gun control. In Chicago alone, there were approximately 1,561 gun-related homicides during his first term of office, a majority of whom were victims of color (Swartz), yet he did not even mention gun violence in his first-term State of the Union addresses. Additionally, gun control and related violence were not topics of discussion during the 2012 presidential campaign, which left the impression that neither candidate wanted to have the gun lobby or the NRA as a potential complication to their respective campaigns. After President Obama's election victory and as a direct result of the Sandy Hook shooting, gun control miraculously became a high-profile presidential priority and was finally addressed in his 2013 State of the Union address—very interesting timing. The Sandy Hook murders also prompted the assignment of Vice President Biden to develop gun-control recommendations, yet again, hundreds of Chicago gun-related homicides only prompted news media footnotes and politically correct "Oh, ain't it awful" proclamations.

During the 2013 State of the Union address, President Obama acknowledged by name various communities affected by gun violence—Newtown, Aurora, Oak Creek, Tucson, and Blacksburg. He never mentioned Chicago or other inner-city, gang-infested locales that had experienced more severe gun violence than the named communities. He acknowledged inner-city and other gun violence with a cursory reference to "the countless *other* communities ripped open by gun violence" (Katz 2013, italics mine). In all fairness, President Obama did mention Detroit in his January 2013 inaugural address and invited Hadiya's parents to the 2013 State of the Union address.

To bolster my argument, there is an historical pattern that extends beyond America's borders. Most notably, during Bill Clinton's presidency, when white-on-white ethnic cleansing and genocide occurred in the majority-white Balkan states of Bosnia and Herzegovina, there was engagement at the highest levels of government with an international intervention that included the deployment of US armed forces to the Balkans—an international version of Sandy Hook. When black-on-black ethnic cleansing and genocide occurred in African states such as the Congo, Uganda, and Rwanda, discussions were relegated to low-level US government officials, and there was no direct US intervention while thousands of Africans were being slaughtered—an international version of Chicago and other inner-city locales. Not surprisingly, the news media colluded with this pattern by giving the Balkans daily and extensive news coverage while Africa received cursory and perfunctory coverage. It apparently did not matter that the death toll in Bosnia and Herzegovina was approximately one hundred thousand, while the death toll in Rwanda alone was between five hundred thousand and one million—a clear indication of racist marginalization and devaluing of the lives of African people of color as compared to white inhabitants of the Balkans.

The similarities between the Balkans/Africa and Sandy Hook/Chicago scenarios are striking, especially with President Obama personally intervening in Sandy Hook on behalf of white children but not in urban inner-city locales on behalf of children of color. Even though President Obama wanted to have a race-neutral presidency, by traveling to Newtown, he enabled the very perception of racism he was hoping to avoid—race-based decision making and preferential treatment. Additionally, President Obama lamented that the Sandy Hook shooting was the worst day of his presidency. In my opinion, he missed the point entirely. The worst days of his presidency should have been Sandy Hook *and* every day Chicago announced its homicide rate, not to mention when other cities announced their respective homicide rates.

More than two months after the Sandy Hook shooting, the news media was still covering the tragedy to include periodically displaying pictures of the murdered children. However, with the exception of Hadiya, I have yet to see a picture of a Chicago child that was murdered in 2012. Children from a Newtown choir sang at the 2013 Super Bowl. How many children's choirs from Chicago ever sang at the Super Bowl?

Lastly, President Obama made a comment during a press conference that if there were any steps that could be taken regarding gun violence to prevent another Sandy Hook, America needs to take those steps. During his 2013 inaugural speech, he made a similar comment that "Our journey is not complete until all our children, from the streets of Detroit to the hills of Appalachia to the quiet lanes of Newtown, know that they are cared for, and cherished, and always safe from harm" (Huffington Post 2013).

I agree with President Obama's sentiments, but I would have hoped for such comments to be made—and action initiated—years earlier, during his first term. Regardless of realities or perceptions, the Sandy Hook shooting sparked long overdue and much-needed national dialogue and action regarding gun violence. Additionally, the "newsworthy" death of Hadiya Pendleton finally focused national and political attention to Chicago's high gun-related homicide rate.

Since I am an African American, it would be fair to ask if my comments are racially motivated—they are not. First, I am a supporter of President Obama, but that does not mean I march lockstep with him on every issue. Second, I point your attention to the TNT medical series *Monday Mornings*. The second episode had scenes that went straight to the heart of my angst about the perceptions of racism associated with the Sandy Hook tragedy. Please bear with me as I explain.

The relevant scenes began in a hospital emergency room with an African American male gang member named Gavin Jasper on a gurney, with part of his head blown away by a gunshot. Since Gavin is an organ donor and initially diagnosed as brain-dead, per protocol, a white transplant surgeon looks for a neurologist to formally declare Gavin brain-dead so his organs can be harvested. It would be a conflict of interest for the transplant surgeon to make such a determination.

The surgeon finds a neurologist and impatiently tries to rush her while she conducts the appropriate tests. Gavin is nonresponsive to all stimuli until the neurologist gives him a verbal command to grasp her hand, and to everyone's shock he does. The surgeon believes it was just an involuntary brain stem reaction, so he instructs Gavin to raise a hand and extend a finger. Gavin raises a hand and flips his middle finger at the surgeon. Mortified, the surgeon storms out of the ER.

Later, the transplant surgeon comes back to the ER and impatiently asks an ER doctor if Gavin is finally dead. He is told that Gavin died, and he expresses relief because he can now harvest Gavin's organs. What the surgeon does not know is that Gavin's mother is sitting next to the ER doctor and she hears everything. Embarrassed, the surgeon apologizes to the mother for his insensitivity and walks away.

After Gavin's organs are harvested, the surgeon runs into Gavin's mother in a waiting room after he enters to tell the white family of the recipient of Gavin's heart that the transplant was a resounding success. After speaking to the family, the surgeon approaches Gavin's mother and again apologizes for his prior insensitivity. He tries to console her by explaining how Gavin's organs helped save the lives of others, such as a school teacher, a doctor, an engineer, a . . . *whack!* The mother slaps the surgeon in the face midsentence and angrily questions the surgeon's motives with a blistering retort—her son was a dying black gang member and his life meant nothing to society or the surgeon, yet when he dies and donates his organs to more "upstanding" (white) people, he is *now* somebody (TNT 2013)?

The reason for the mother's outrage should be obvious and is another example of fiction mirroring reality. A black gang member is killed and it is "business as usual," yet impact white people and the game changes radically. Consequently, my opinions did not emanate from a racial bias. I reacted to indisputable homicide statistics and social behaviors that expose an obvious racist reality in America—skin color still dominates social behaviors and decision making.

In closing, do murdered children need to be white to jumpstart national attention and action? It would appear so. If Sandy Hook had not occurred, would the resulting debate on gun control have been initiated? Would Hadiya have received national attention? Again, perception can be a person's reality, and given the perception of racism in this instance, it should not be a surprise if African Americans continue to ask: *How does my country really feel about me?*

Voter Suppression

An appropriate rendition of "The King is dead. Long live the King" would be "Jim Crow is dead. Long live Jim Crow." In other words, just as a king or queen dies and a successor ascends to the throne, a manifestation of racism like poll taxes and literary tests may die, but another takes its place—such as contemporary voter suppression.

After the Constitution was adopted, only rich, white, male property owners had the right to vote—omitting women, slaves, and the poor. Voting was eventually expanded to other groups of men, but suppressing the vote of free African Americans and women continued. Women finally won the right to vote in 1920, but voting prerequisites such as literacy tests and poll taxes targeted and further disenfranchised African Americans, especially in southern states.

Poll taxes and similar voting restrictions were finally lifted by the 1964 ratification of the twenty-fourth amendment and the 1965 Voting Rights Act (Hudson 2012). However, if at first you do not succeed, try, try again, which is exactly what GOP state lawmakers tried to do during the 2012 general election. Under the dubious guise of preventing alleged voter fraud, several GOP-led state legislatures restricted or limited aspects of the voting process, resulting in some legislation or executive actions being ruled unconstitutional in various state and federal courts. Seventeen states passed restrictive voting laws that had the potential to affect the 2012 election. These states accounted for 218 electoral votes, or nearly 80 percent of the total needed to win the presidency. These GOP-led efforts imposed a series of new restrictions on voting such as strict new voter-ID laws, limits on voter-registration drives, and closing early-voting windows, which created fewer voting precincts and longer lines (Hudson 2012).

Considering the heightened number of Hispanic and African American voters and their potential impact on election outcomes, the GOP using voter suppression as a means to stymie the reelection bid of President Obama came as no surprise. The GOP was keenly aware that an overwhelming majority of minority voters were aligned with the Democratic Party. Not surprisingly, GOP-generated allegations of voter fraud did not stand up to official scrutiny. Regardless of the GOP's rationale for enacting restrictive voting protocols, it reeked of racially motivated attempts to circumvent the Voting Rights Act. Regarding voter suppression activities in Florida, assertions by former heads of Florida's GOP Charlie Crist and Jim Greer seem to validate my conclusions. Along with Greer's concerns, Crist had this to say:

> People have fought and died for our right to vote, and unfortunately our legislature and this governor have decided they want to make early voting less available to Floridians rather than more available . . . It's hard for me as an American to comprehend why you don't make democracy as easy as possible to exercise for the people of our state. It's frankly unconscionable. (Grey 2012)

In 2013, there was a US Supreme Court appeal to Section 5 of the 1965 Voting Rights Act. Section 5 required all or parts of sixteen states, with a history of racial discrimination, to get approval from the Justice Department or a federal court before making changes in the way they hold elections, such as moving a polling place. This provision was enacted due to past discrimination against African, Native, and Asian Americans, Alaskan natives, and Hispanics, and applied to Alabama, Alaska, Arizona, Georgia, Louisiana, Mississippi, South Carolina, Texas, and Virginia. It also covered various jurisdictions in California, Florida, New York, North Carolina, South Dakota, Michigan, and New Hampshire (Superville 2013).

During oral arguments, Justice Scalia asked if Section 5 was a racial entitlement and not a constitutional necessity. Later, while referring to the unanimous US Senate vote in 2006 to extend the Voting Rights Act, Scalia added that it was "very likely attributable to a phenomenon that is called perpetuation of racial entitlement. It's been written about.

Whenever a society adopts racial entitlements, it is very difficult to get out of them through the normal political processes" (Troutt 2013).

Given his conservative inclinations, Scalia's comments were shocking, but not surprising, prompting some critics to believe Justice Scalia is a racist. I am not sure if his comments emanated from racist inclinations or he was playing the role of a judicial provocateur, as he has done on previous occasions. However, Scalia's description of the Voting Rights Act as a "racial entitlement" gives me pause and warrants clarification.

In a 5–4 decision, the Supreme Court ruled that Section 4 of the Voting Rights Act was unconstitutional until Congress developed a new way of determining which states and municipalities require close federal election monitoring. The court said the Voting Rights Act relied on outdated data not reflective of racial progress in America. By throwing out Section 4, the court negated the enforcement power of Section 5, thus neutralizing the heart of the Voting Rights Act (Liptak 2013).

Despite Scalia's comments and given the court's ruling, to stop voter suppression attempts in the future, we should update Section 4 and expand the Voting Rights Act by mandating generic nationwide protocols dictating how general elections will be conducted, such as allowable poll hours, early-voting parameters, and identification requirements. Include requirements for allowable methods of voting, such as in-person, e-mail, provisional, and absentee ballots. Given the current GOP majority in the House of Representatives, enacting such changes would be problematic.

Lastly, we should enforce the Voting Rights Act on behalf of minorities and whites alike. Voting rights violations against white voters should be prosecuted with the same vigor as violations against voters of color. In the meantime, Americans need to stop electing lawmakers responsible for thinly veiled attempts to maintain a racial status-quo versus protecting the voting rights of all Americans.

Wealth, Power, and "Forty Acres and a Mule"

Since overt acts of racism are illegal in America, racism has mutated into a form that leverages the institutional power of the checkbook and pen. This mutation has resulted in racism's ability to control access to wealth and power, thus becoming the contemporary means to keep

African Americans in a lingering state of socioeconomic and political bankruptcy. Many African Americans still operate at a deficit and are conditioned to expect only "forty acres and a mule" rather than the full benefits of the American Dream. Let's examine this premise further.

—Wealth

Wealth is a financial measure of worth, but how it is controlled and distributed is a measure of what is truly valued. From this perspective, let's examine wealth among African Americans. Historically, there have only been two African American billionaires, Bob Johnson (founder of Black Entertainment Television) and Oprah Winfrey (Harpo Productions owner and talk show hostess). As of mid-2012, there were approximately 425 billionaires in America, with Oprah Winfrey as the only remaining African American billionaire ("Black Billionaires"). On a corroborating note, according to US Census Bureau figures, the median household net worth for white Americans was $110,729 in 2010 versus $4,995 for African Americans (Tami Luhby 2012). There is a saying that "money talks," yet it appears the conversation does not include African Americans or African American households. Why is this?

Wealth gives the wealthy a heightened sense of entitlement and privilege. With exceptions, such as philanthropist billionaires Bill Gates and Warren Buffett, the wealthy is against wealth distribution, and apathetic and unsympathetic to the widening gap between the rich, middle class, and poor. Since a majority of wealthy Americans are white, add racism to the equation, it is easy to understand why African Americans have historically been at or near the bottom of America's wealth pyramid.

The first attempt to distribute wealth to African Americans was in 1865. "Forty acres and a mule" was a phrase describing a policy that provided small parcels of land to former slaves who were freed as a result of Union Civil War victories in territories previously controlled by the Confederacy. General Sherman's Special Field Orders, No. 15, provided the land, with some former slaves receiving plow mules— hence the phrase "forty acres and a mule." However, President Andrew Johnson revoked Sherman's order and returned the confiscated land to its previous white owners ("Forty Acres and a Mule").

Regarding equitable opportunities to realize wealth in present-day America, African Americans continue to lag behind white counterparts with only "forty acres and a mule" to show for their efforts. Current exceptions are the few African American millionaires in professional sports, corporate America, and the entertainment industry, as well as lottery winners, with most lacking in influential socioeconomic or political power.

—Power

The ancient Greek philosopher Plato warned that access to power must be confined to those who are not in love with it. Even though Plato was referring to an individual's access to and love of power, his warning could also apply to racism's access to and love of power.

Again, as of the end of 2012, there are only six African American CEOs in the Fortune 500 companies. Barack Obama was one of eight African American US senators in history before becoming the first African American president of the United States. There have been only two African American secretaries of state and national security advisors; both positions held by Colin Powell and Condoleezza Rice. There has only been one African American chairman of the Joint Chiefs of Staff, Colin Powell, and one African American US attorney general, Eric Holder. The US Supreme Court has only had two African American justices, Thurgood Marshall and Clarence Thomas.

In the 111th Congress, there were only four African American house committee chairpersons and one US senator (Black Americans in Congress). In the 112th Congress, there were no African American senators or congressional committee chairpersons. Let's not even discuss the minuscule number of African American ambassadors (with the exception of ambassadors to African countries and ambassador to the UN Susan Rice) or cabinet-level secretaries in America's history. In the private sector, civil-rights activist Vernon Jordan was a very influential and powerful African American advisor to President Clinton. Finally, as of the end of 2012 and with the exceptions of Oprah Winfrey and current African American Fortune 500 CEOs, I cannot name one legitimate African American power broker in the private sector.

—"Forty Acres and a Mule"

Despite overwhelming economic potential, African Americans still do not invest in their own communities as other cultures do as a matter of course and, with the exceptions of the 2008 and 2012 general elections, do not coalesce into formidable voting blocks to influence elections or protect their interests—both indicative of an embedded "forty acres and a mule" mentality. Again, why is this?

As a culture, African Americans do not have an empowering and enabling sense of community, tradition, or heritage as other cultures have historically maintained and perpetuated. African American cultural norms, social behaviors, and expressions of ethnic and individual self-esteem were formed under the direct influence of slavery and Jim Crow, not from family and cultural traditions emanating from ancestral homelands such as Africa. For example:

- Similar to the renaming of Kunta Kinte to Toby Waller (a main character in Alex Haley's book *Roots*), a slave's birth name was changed to a white name that included the slave owner's last name. This practice, along with the constant breakup of family structures due to family members being sold, makes it virtually impossible for most present-day African Americans to trace their family lineage back more than a few generations. This prompts discussions about the impacts of not having ancestral ties or family or cultural traditions on the prevalence of matriarchal single-parent African American families, and less-than-nurturing relationships between African American men and women.
- African Americans use the n-word in song, rap, comedy, film, and private interactions. As slaves were forced to take on slave-master names, did racism also indoctrinate African Americans into accepting the n-word as an appropriate racial descriptor, thus legitimizing the marginalization of black self-esteem? In other words, does the African American use of the n-word, a racial slur created by antebellum slave owners and propagated by Jim Crow racists, indicate a continuation of a slave mentality and the perpetuation of a racist reality African Americans have been fighting to overcome? These questions prompted me to stop using the n-word and all other racial slurs.
- It was forbidden for slaves to learn or be taught how to read and write. These prohibitions morphed into a Jim Crow system that blocked African American access to quality education, job opportunities and advancement, and other basic civil rights by

establishing restrictive socioeconomic and political glass ceilings. These ceilings have since been cracked, but not shattered.

- Social hierarchies and measures of individual worth and self-esteem were based on whether a slave labored in the slave owner's home or in the fields or was light- or dark-skinned, not individual economic, social, or political accomplishments. Tangentially, this raises an interesting question as to why, during black-initiated race riots of the 1960s to present day, African Americans invariably destroyed their own and other minority-owned properties (the fields), yet with few exceptions, never extended the violence into nearby white communities (slave owner homes).

- The common practice of white males raping black women resulted in mulattos (one white and one black parent), quadroons (one-quarter black ancestry), octoroons (one-eighth black ancestry), and so on. This added to individual and cultural confusion, and the loss of family identities among slaves and their postslavery descendants. As is the case with many contemporary African American family structures such as mine, the white part of our family ancestry will remain unknown or closed to us.

- Many biracial and multiracial former slaves and their descendants were and still are excluded from the fruits of inheritance and fair distribution of the estates of white ancestors, as well as reparations for slavery. The uncertainty of African American family lineages is one of many complications resulting in these exclusions. This uncertainty was magnified due to the lack of birth and death certificates for slaves.

- Regarding reparations, Japanese Americans received reparations for their internment during WWII, and Jews received reparations from Germany for the Holocaust; yet slavery, an atrocity arguably far worse than forced internment and longer-lasting than the Holocaust, only warranted an apology from Congress and various states. Keep in mind that President Andrew Johnson started this ball rolling by revoking General Sherman's Special Field Orders, No. 15, and confiscating the "forty acres and a mule" given to emancipated slaves, thus denying former slaves even the paltriest of reparations for centuries of slavery.

How do I feel about myself and my country? Are African Americans still puppets, with racism as the puppeteer?

Who Controls the Fountains?

It is now the twenty-first century, and African Americans have yet to escape from under Plymouth Rock. Among too many African Americans, there is still a lack of positive cultural self-actualization that results in expectations of disenfranchisement, second-class-citizen status, and marginal achievement levels. African Americans still bear racism's yoke and remain in a deficit regarding wealth accumulation and obtaining meaningful political, social, and financial power. Malcolm X cut to the chase with two sentences: "We didn't land on Plymouth Rock. The rock was landed on us" (YouTube 2006).

America's racial climate has greatly improved, but America has a long way to go before it can be said that it is truly a country where all people of color have equal opportunities to pursue and consume the rich and power-laden fruits of the American Dream. Additionally, African Americans have a long way to go before we can call ourselves a legitimate and cohesive culture versus disparate individuals of the same color.

Herman Cain told a story about when, as adolescents, he and his brother approached White Only and Colored Only water fountains in segregated Georgia. When they noticed that no one was looking, they drank from both fountains, looked at each other, and bragged, "The water tastes the same. What's the big deal?" ("Herman Cain").

They both missed the point. The "big deal" was not their ability to drink the water. It was racism's power to control access to the water fountains because, for all of their bravado, they would not have drunk from the White Only water fountain if a white person was watching— the real moral to the story. In the same regard, the issues are not having wealth and power, but racism's ability to control access to them.

As African Americans, we need to relearn how to demand and protect our rights and, regardless of who is "watching the water fountains," acquire equal access to all American Dream fountains so we do not perish from the earth due to racism-induced cultural dehydration or, as Malcolm X proclaimed, "We declare our right on this earth . . .

to be a human being, to be respected as a human being, to be given the rights of a human being in this society, on this earth, in this day, which we intend to bring into existence *by any means necessary*" (Malcolm-X. org).

Zimmerman: The Last Straw?

Having discussed specific aspects of racism in America, how do I summarize racism in general? How do I explain the racial fears, stereotypes, and suspicions that are deeply embedded in black and white psyches and the depression, anger, and frustration African Americans feel while enduring racism in a country where all men and women are supposed to be created and considered equal?

In recent times, nothing has illuminated racism and crystallized its impacts more than the George Zimmerman and Trayvon Martin tragedy, in which a Hispanic (Zimmerman) shot and killed an unarmed black teenager (Trayvon)—a tragedy I discuss in detail in chapter 2, "Justice." Zimmerman was charged with second-degree murder, a trial ensued, and he was acquitted. His acquittal sparked an emotional nationwide debate and protest demonstrations. Was Zimmerman killing Trayvon the last straw?

As part of the debate, I sent an e-mail to friends that shared thoughts about the Zimmerman trial and racism in general. Below are relevant portions of my e-mail:

> Regardless of whether or not Zimmerman shot and killed Trayvon Martin with racist intent, African Americans are so tired of being continually hit by racism's pitches, Zimmerman's intent no longer matters. Zimmerman killing Trayvon was the trigger and the last straw, rekindling memories of the Jim Crow era when a white person was never convicted for killing a black person in almost all southern state courts, or the continual and present-day profiling and stereotyping of African Americans. Ironically, Zimmerman is not white. He is [biracial] Hispanic or "brown" on the ethnic color scale; however, he could pass as white, which was probably another factor fueling the backlash. . . .

Was the Zimmerman case an example of prototypical racism? Contrary to popular belief, absolutely not. In my opinion, race had nothing to do with Zimmerman's or Trayvon's actions. However, was the Zimmerman case emblematic of racism in America? Yes, and this is all that matters. What the Zimmerman case symbolizes goes to the heart of African American frustration and anger—the continued and racist marginalization of African Americans in every aspect of America's socioeconomic infrastructure, whether by overt or institutional racism—all fueled by racial fears and stereotypes, and with the intent of keeping African Americans at a deficit.

A white-looking Hispanic man tragically kills a black boy, thus tipping the scale of already boiling anger; however, I wonder what the reaction would've been if Zimmerman was black—probably no reaction whatsoever. Why? African Americans are also tired of black/brown-on-black/brown crime, gang violence, and homicides being treated as business as usual or the status quo of inner-city life, thus marginalizing the intrinsic value of black and brown lives, and perpetuating the cycle of violence where youth of color are victims and perpetrators of violence. . . .

I could go on and on, but I think you get the point. Again, the Zimmerman case was not about race, but it became racial (hope this makes sense). In my opinion, if you dig down to the true source of the anger, African Americans are not as upset with Zimmerman as they are upset with the system that allowed him to criminally[or racially] profile Trayvon and pull the trigger.

As evidenced by the Zimmerman case, despite an improved racial environment and laws that delegitimize most overt forms of racism, the civil rights struggle will continue because when one form of racism dies, another takes its place—Jim Crow is dead, long live Jim Crow. As such, how do I effectively summarize racism? Consider the following:

- Racism is no longer about segregation, antimiscegenation laws, and overt acts of violence by anonymous whites in white sheets. As in the Zimmerman case, racism has become more sophisticated by hiding behind state laws, such as Stand Your Ground and concealed carry laws, that perpetuate the cycles of crime, gun violence, and homicides that decimate black and Hispanic youth and adversely affect their communities.

- Racism no longer has the influence, especially in southern state courts, to provide blanket protection for white perpetrators of violence against blacks. Racism now influences a criminal justice system that continues the disproportionate incarceration and executions of African Americans.

- Racism can no longer prevent African Americans from living in white or affluent neighborhoods via exclusionary practices such as real estate covenants. It now focuses on intimidating African Americans and Hispanics who drive or walk through neighborhoods via profiling by the police and ordinary citizens and stop-and-frisk policies.

- Racism can no longer disallow African Americans from eating in restaurants or drinking water from water fountains that were once designated as White Only. It now focuses on excluding African Americans from access to and partaking of the economic fruits of the American Dream, relegating African Americans to just "forty acres and a mule."

- Racism is no longer about preventing African Americans from being hired into or promoted within corporate and similar institutions. It now creates racist glass ceilings that prevent most African Americans from achieving executive leadership positions that change organizational culture and manage wealth.

- Racism can no longer restrict participation in the voting process via poll taxes and literacy tests. It now impedes participation through subtler mechanisms such as voter suppression—legal acts or laws that make it difficult for African Americans and other Americans of color to identify themselves at voting sites, or to get to voting sites on time or at all.

- Racism can no longer prevent the election of African American US presidents or members of Congress. It now focuses on limiting African American access to influential congressional committee chairs and related leadership positions, and gerrymandering congressional district boundaries to the electoral and political disadvantages of African Americans.

Again, how do I summarize racism? Racism is a robust and evolving parasitic anathema that infests every aspect of American life. Until the curse of racism is permanently exorcised from America's ethos, America will never truly be the land of the free, and African Americans and other Americans of color will never fully enjoy life, liberty, or the pursuit of happiness.

Chapter 2

JUSTICE

How does my country feel about me?

"The benchmark of a civilized society is the quality of its justice" (Waterston, *Law and Order* [Episode: "Thinking Makes It So"] 2006). Accordingly, the promise of equal justice for all is backed by the full power of the Constitution; however, constitutional promises and actual practice do not always coincide. In this regard, I will be discussing the following areas of concern:

- Civil and Criminal Standards of Proof
- Death Penalty
- Guilty Until Proven Innocent
- Paying for an Attorney
- Right to Privacy
- "The Jury Will Disregard . . ."
- Tort Reform
- Torture and Indefinite Detention
- US Supreme Court Appointments

Not being a jurist or legal scholar puts me at a disadvantage constructing this discussion in the complicated language and formats used by the judicial system. Who knows Latin *pro se* from *hearsay*? Please keep this caveat in mind as you continue to read.

Civil and Criminal Standards of Proof

Currently, it is possible for a defendant to be acquitted in criminal court, yet held liable for similar charges in civil court. For example, OJ Simpson was acquitted of murder in criminal court but held liable in civil court for wrongful death. This practice is unfair and should be considered double jeopardy and unconstitutional.

In criminal cases, "beyond a reasonable doubt" is the mandated standard of proof required for convictions. In civil cases, the standard of proof is much lower; based on "proof by a preponderance of the evidence" or "proof by clear and convincing evidence" (Standler 2002). The US Supreme Court agrees with this standard of proof distinction; however, I passionately disagree. There should only be one standard of proof for both criminal and civil cases.

Criminal trials have a higher standard of proof because in addition to fines, restitution, and possible loss of property, convicted defendants can face incarceration and possible execution while civil defendants only face penalties such as money damages and injunctive relief. Incarceration and execution are not within the purview of civil courts. In other words, the commonly held distinction between criminal and civil trials is their relative impact on a defendant's right to life, liberty, and the pursuit of happiness.

The unalienable rights to life, liberty, and the pursuit of happiness are human rights that are absolute and should not be denied without due process of law. These rights can be taken away or impeded if criminal or civil laws are violated. The ability of courts to impact our unalienable rights should require the highest level of proof regardless of whether the possible punishment is life in prison for a crime or five million dollars in civil damages. The severity of the punishment a court can administer should have no bearing on the legal standards used to prove criminal guilt or civil liability. The focus of the court should be the equitable protection of unalienable rights.

Equal justice under law should also mean equal legal standards such as the standard of proof. If there was only one standard of proof, facing a civil trial after an acquittal or dismissal with prejudice in criminal court would be theoretically disallowed under the double jeopardy rule. Any criminal or civil impediment on a defendant's right to life, liberty, and pursuit of happiness should be adjudicated under the highest legal standard of proof—guilty or liable beyond a reasonable doubt.

Currently in civil court, the right to pursue happiness can be impeded by a jury or judge who has an educated hunch the defendant is liable versus being sure beyond a reasonable doubt. Using hypothetical percentages to provide context, I wonder how Americans really feel about being judged based on a standard of proof mandating a minimal 51 percent level of certainty in civil court as compared to a 90-plus percent level of certainty in criminal cases.

If there was a single standard of proof, beyond a reasonable doubt, in both courts, a defendant convicted in criminal court could still be sued in civil court; however, civil liability would already be legally established by the criminal conviction. The only tasks for the civil court would be to determine the levels of liability and award appropriate damages. This could lead to another benefit. The average time for a civil case to get to the trial phase is approximately two to three years. Small Claims Court litigation is the exception, with most cases being resolved in a few months or less. If civil trials against defendants acquitted in criminal court were shortened, the length of time it takes for civil cases to be heard and adjudicated would also be shortened.

America's justice system is designed to be fair and equitable. If America is truly about equal justice under law, then this must be reinforced by equal legal standards of proof used to determine criminal guilt and civil liability.

Death Penalty

I support the death penalty and will not discuss its pros and cons; however, I have concerns with (1) the time it takes to execute someone, (2) US Supreme Court Justices Scalia's and Thomas's assertion that the claim of actual innocence may not be "constitutionally cognizable," and (3) the standard of proof required for a guilty verdict in a capital case.

An American citizen has the constitutional right to a speedy trial. The same principle should apply to the speedy execution of sentences. However, because of a protracted appeals process, once a convicted defendant is sentenced to death, it can take ten to thirty years before he or she is executed. This is cruel and unusual punishment not only for the condemned inmate, but also for the family and loved ones of the homicide victims who are waiting for justice to finally be done. Additionally, the costs to incarcerate a prisoner on Death Row for decades coupled with the cost of the appeals process are astronomical.

Looking at the appeals process, I am confused and disturbed by Scalia's and Thomas's "constitutionally cognizable" assertion, as it applies to hearing appeals based on claims of actual innocence. Their logic appears to advocate disregarding appeals based on claims of actual innocence if the petitioner received a fair trial.

On a different note, the death penalty can be imposed after a guilty verdict for a capital crime. To minimize the possibility of executing an innocent person, the death penalty should not be applied unless there is a guilty verdict based on the highest possible standard of proof—guilty to a reasonable certainty—a standard of proof that currently does not, but should exist.

Appeals Process

The death penalty appeals process is way too long. There is a saying that justice delayed is justice denied, a legal maxim that can be attributed to the Magna Carta. The Magna Carta established rights for thirteenth-century noblemen and ordinary Englishmen, as well as the principle that no one, including a king or queen, was above the law. Clause 40 of the Magna Carta stated, "To no one will we sell, to no one will we refuse *or delay*, right or justice" (Constitution Society 2013, italics mine).

One way to resolve the problem of protracted death penalty appeals would be to replace the death penalty with life in prison without parole; however, the death penalty is still in force in federal, military, and many state legal systems. As such, I will continue this discussion under the assumption that the death penalty will be in effect for the foreseeable future.

One reason for the elongated appeals process is that the same state and federal courts of appeal that hear death penalty appeals must also adjudicate all other civil and criminal appeals. The highest level of judicial appeal is the US Supreme Court, and it only reviews a handful of death penalty appeals a year. In other words, with the exception of emergency appeals to avert imminent executions, death penalty appeals must wait their turn in a court's docket. Since there are three-thousand-plus inmates currently on Death Row, it becomes intuitively obvious why a protracted appeals process is unavoidable and extremely costly; however, there may be a way to speed up the process.

Establish state and federal death penalty courts of appeal whose sole purpose is to hear death penalty appeals. There are precedents for such courts. In civil litigation, Small Claims Court quickly resolves cases involving damages of approximately $5,000 or less, thus allowing higher-level courts to focus on more complicated and time-consuming cases involving greater damages. There are many other examples of state and federal courts that focus on one specific aspect of the law, such as Family and Administrative courts.

The Constitution authorizes Congress to define the organization of the federal court system, and I am assuming that state constitutions provide similar authority for the establishment of state court systems. A Death Penalty Court would mirror its respective counterpart in composition and authority: the State Appellate Court and State Death Penalty Appellate Court, US District Court and US District Death Penalty Court, US Court of Appeals and US Death Penalty Court of Appeals, and the US Supreme Court and US Death Penalty Supreme Court. Obviously, a duplicate set of federal judges would need to be appointed. The Constitution requires federal court judges to be appointed by the president of the United States and approved by the US Senate; however, mitigating the delays in and costs of the death penalty appeals process and accompanying high cost of incarcerating condemned inmates would be worth the effort and cost to empanel such courts.

Again, justice delayed is justice denied.

Executing an Innocent Person

In 2011, Troy Anthony Davis was executed for the murder of a police officer after exhausting all appeals. Prior to his execution, evidence surfaced that suggested his innocence. When his appeal reached the US Supreme Court, Justices Scalia and Thomas basically stated that mere innocence is not grounds to overturn a conviction or even hear the case. With Scalia and Thomas in dissent, the majority opinion gave Davis the opportunity to appeal. The dissenting opinion read in part:

> This Court has *never* held that the Constitution forbids the execution of a convicted defendant who has had a full and fair trial, but is later able to convince a habeas court that he is

"actually" innocent. Quite to the contrary, we have repeatedly left that question unresolved, while expressing considerable doubt that any claim based on alleged "actual innocence" is constitutionally cognizable. (Scalia and Thomas 2009)

Apparently, by Scalia's and Thomas's assessments, the law has no problem with executing an innocent person as long as he or she received a fair trial. Since an execution is irreversible and the harshest of all criminal penalties, this logic is hard to fathom and very disturbing. They were basically stating that, based on the lack of constitutional or judicial precedent, appellate courts should not consider cases concerning the execution of a potentially innocent person—again, as long as he or she received a full and fair trial.

As another example of fiction mirroring reality, in an episode of the TV series *Law and Order*, Executive Assistant District Attorney Jack McCoy receives exculpatory evidence that proves the innocence of a person serving a prison term. McCoy presents this evidence to the District Attorney responsible for the case. The DA refuses to take action because the prisoner received a fair trial and a legally sufficient jury conviction and sentence (Waterston and David, *Law and Order* [Episode: "Bronx Cheer"] 2001). In other words, actual innocence was not sufficient enough to overcome a guilty verdict, or worse, protecting the judicial process was more important than protecting the prisoner's constitutional rights—a very dangerous proposition.

The Constitution does not specifically address executions, but at some point, the literal interpretation of the Constitution must give way to common sense and, regarding death penalty cases, err on the side of caution. Again, the Declaration of Independence clearly states that all Americans have the unalienable rights to life, liberty, and the pursuit of happiness. The Fifth and Fourteenth Amendments of the Constitution ensure that a citizen cannot lose any of these rights without due process of law.

If, after a capital conviction, there is credible evidence to show the possibility of a flaw in the original determination of guilt, it should be a constitutional right for the accused to challenge the conviction in a court of law, and in the case of a pending execution, the execution should *always* be stayed until the new evidence can be reviewed by the appropriate appellate court and a new judgment rendered. An erroneous noncapital conviction can be reversed, but an execution cannot.

If someone is executed and later found to be innocent, the responsible state or federal entity may have committed an unconstitutional act and should be held legally accountable. This possibility, along with the possibility of executing an innocent person, should make all death penalty appeals based on a claim of actual innocence constitutionally cognizable. The fact that there was a fair trial or lack of precedent should have no bearing on decisions to hear such appeals.

Standard of Proof

Previously, I argued for a "beyond a reasonable doubt" standard of proof for both criminal and civil trials; however, the finality of an execution prompts the one exception to my previous standard-of-proof proposal.

Technological advances, such as the advent of DNA and related forensic capabilities, raise the possibility that, prior to these advances, an innocent person may have been executed. A significant number of prisoners have been exonerated due to DNA testing that was not available when they were convicted. However, when one is executed, there is no future exoneration—he or she is dead. Since the death penalty is the most severe and irreversible of all criminal penalties, a guilty verdict resulting in a sentence of death should correspondently carry the highest and most stringent standard of proof—"guilty to a reasonable certainty." As compared to a reasonable doubt verdict, a reasonable certainty verdict would greatly decrease the possibility of executing an innocent person. In many jurisdictions, there are precedents for different burdens of proof. In insanity defenses in criminal court, the burden of proof shifts from the prosecution to the defense, and there are several circumstances where the burden of proof shifts to the defendant in civil cases. If the burden of proof can change until select circumstances, why can't a standard of proof also change for a capital case?

Because "reasonable certainty" and "reasonable doubt" are subjective measures, and given the extent of human understanding and technology, definitively quantifying reasonable doubt or certainty is still beyond current intellectual and scientific capabilities, but they both can be defined in a manner that is consistent with current human levels of perception and understanding, and the technology available. This said, the criteria for a reasonable certainty conviction must include an overwhelming preponderance of evidence, such as, but not limited to, a preponderance of *consistent* and *credible* eye witness testimony, the availability of *irrefutable* video and sound technology that records the crime or spontaneous admissions of guilt, or uncontested confessions, i.e., the evidence should leave absolutely no doubt in the jury's mind that the defendant committed the crime. A conviction based solely on circumstantial or DNA evidence may be sufficient for a "beyond a reasonable doubt" conviction, but would not be considered reasonable certainty and would not be eligible for death sentence consideration. In summary, the difference between a reasonable doubt verdict and a reasonable certainty verdict would be the amount, quality, and type of evidence.

Additionally, a reasonable certainty verdict should be unanimous. If one juror votes guilty beyond a reasonable doubt, but not to a reasonable certainty, a death sentence should not be considered. Under such a circumstance, the maximum allowable sentence would be life without parole. Requiring unanimity would be aligned with current precedent in most capital cases. With the exceptions of Alabama and Florida, a unanimous jury verdict is required to impose the death penalty during state capital trials. All federal criminal trials require a unanimous verdict.

A reasonable certainty standard of proof will not guarantee that an innocent person will never be executed. The error that still exists in current forensic and other investigative technologies precludes such a guarantee—a major limitation to my argument. Requiring a reasonable certainty standard of proof is one thing; developing legally sufficient criteria for such a standard is another. If criteria for a reasonable certainty standard of proof cannot be developed and applied, the heightened possibility of executing an innocent person under a lower standard of proof should result in erring on the side of caution by not rendering a death sentence. As a final conclusion, if it is not possible to develop appropriate criteria for reasonable certainty, the death penalty should be eliminated.

Guilty Until Proven Innocent

In America, an accused person is supposed to be presumed innocent until proven guilty in a court of law. The news media and celebrity pundits such as Nancy Grace need to be reminded of this legal principle because, apparently, their approach is guilty until proven innocent. Steve Brill, the creator of *Court TV*, made this point very clear while criticizing Grace:

> In an interview with the AP's David Bauder, Brill called Grace a "monster," and not in a good way. "I feel like I owe the nation community service for having hired her and put her on television. She's a monster," Brill said.
>
> Brill added that the point of *Court TV* reporters and experts is to inform viewers and clarify the legal process, not to offer opinions about guilt or innocence. (TVNewser 2011)

The presumption of innocence until proven guilty is one of the most important principles in America's system of justice. However, this principle is not actually written in the Constitution, but is embodied in several provisions such as the right to have legal counsel, to have a jury trial, and to remain silent. To reinforce this, a maxim in criminal law states that it is far worse to convict one innocent person than to let ten guilty persons go free.

The media operates under its own rules. Too many times, the media takes inappropriate license with the presumption of innocence by communicating alleged offenses while implying guilt with their analysis. Thanks to Nancy Grace and other pundits, in their zeal to report the news, the accused is tried and convicted in the court of public opinion before an actual trial occurs. This amounts to an egregious violation of the accused's privacy and defamation of his or her character by implication or direct accusation—all without a judgment in a court of law. For example, after unrelenting public accusations and malicious judgments of guilt by Nancy Grace, on her television crime show, two of her targets committed suicide. In my opinion, Grace was judge, jury, and executioner.

Prior to Jerry Sandusky's conviction for child molestation and related felonies, Nancy Colasurdo, a practicing life coach and freelance writer, criticized the Sandusky news coverage by saying, "Every day in the news there's something that sends us to that rush, rush, rush to judgment. From grave to petty to disappointing" (Colasurdo 2012).

This is so true, and sadly the media's behavior is legal under the protection of the First Amendment. A rush to judgment also occurred in the media treatment of OJ Simpson, Dominique Strauss-Kahn, and others. What if Simpson and Strauss-Kahn were actually innocent?

To present a clearer picture of the media's typical rush to judgment, consider the past and current cases regarding Tawana Brawley and Trayvon Martin, respectively.

Tawana Brawley

A classic example of media abuse was the rush to judgment in the 1987 case of an African American teenager from New York—Tawana Brawley. At age fifteen, she received national media attention for accusing six white police officers of raping her. These accusations reignited decades-old racial hostilities that were inflamed by Tawana's advisors, such as Rev. Al Sharpton, public officials, and the intense media attention.

Tawana's advisors claimed local and state government officials were trying to cover up for the defendants because they were white. They even accused a New York Assistant District Attorney of being one of the rapists. The mainstream news media's coverage drew well-deserved criticism for its malicious treatment of Tawana and the appearance of participating in the alleged cover-up. Several violations of Tawana's privacy were cited, such as the publication of photos taken of her at the hospital and revealing her name despite Tawana being underage. This only served to add fuel to the fire for a rush to judgment and premature guilty verdict by the African American community and many others. Then, the grand jury convened.

The grand jury concluded that Tawana had not been the victim of a sexual assault and may have created the appearance of an attack. Tawana later told others that there had been no rape; only other kinds of sexual abuse. Forensic tests found no evidence of a sexual assault or exposure to the elements, which would have been expected in a victim held for several days in the woods when the temperature was sometimes below freezing. Additionally, there was evidence to suggest that Tawana had a motive to fabricate the rape because she may have feared a severe beating at home for staying out too late. Needless to say, the grand jury's conclusions decreased support for Tawana and her advisers, and a decade later, the New York prosecutor successfully sued Tawana, Rev. Sharpton, and two of her advisors for defamation ("Tawana Brawley Rape Allegations"). Tawana still maintains the allegations were true, but what if she lied?

I struggled with this question because I was part of the problem. In reaction to the news media's abuse of Tawana and out of frustration for the tendency to sweep white-on-black crime under the rug, in my mind I convicted the alleged rapists before the grand jury convened. I did not extend to the accused the presumption of innocence. As an outspoken advocate of civil liberties, the blatant hypocrisy of criticizing the news media and pundits while proclaiming Tawana's alleged assailants guilty until proven innocent did not escape me—a realization that prompted a more constitutionally appropriate approach on my part while following the Trayvon Martin case.

Trayvon Martin

Trayvon Martin was a seventeen-year-old African American teenager shot to death in 2012 by George Zimmerman, a Hispanic neighborhood watch volunteer in Florida. Zimmerman claimed he fired in self-defense after Trayvon attacked him and was protected by Florida's Stand Your Ground law that allowed him to use deadly force if he feared he was in imminent danger of losing his life or incurring grave bodily harm. In my opinion, the news media and many in the general public tried and convicted Zimmerman without all the evidence and, most egregiously, before a trial. He should have been presumed innocent until proven guilty in a court of law; however, he was not afforded this presumption.

Based on pictures allegedly provided by the Martin family legal team and without due diligence, the news media inaccurately depicted Trayvon as a shorter and skinnier twelve- to fifteen-year-old versus the five-foot-eleven seventeen-year-old he actually was during the altercation. When the outdated pictures of Trayvon were aired,

Zimmerman's need to resort to deadly force with such a young, unassuming, and "wimpy-looking kid" was called into question, thus, in my opinion, contributing to the groundswell of protest demonstrations and rushes to judgment. When current pictures of Trayvon were eventually aired, it became immediately obvious how five-foot-seven Zimmerman could have been threatened and manhandled by a teenager who was taller, older, and heavier than originally depicted.

Prior to Zimmerman's arrest, continuous news media coverage of what seemed to be biased and questionable exhortations by the Martin family legal team further contributed to the widespread emotional and racial fervor against Zimmerman. Similar to his actions in the Tawana Brawley case, Rev. Al Sharpton organized anti-Zimmerman protest demonstrations in Florida. Celebrity movie director Spike Lee maliciously tweeted the wrong Zimmerman address, resulting in the occupants having to evacuate their home out of fear for their lives. Similarly, celebrity actress Roseanne Barr allegedly tweeted Zimmerman's parents' correct address, forcing his parents to leave their home. The New Black Panther Party offered a $10,000 bounty for the citizen's arrest of Zimmerman. This bounty was ill-timed and totally inappropriate, because if anyone forcibly detained Zimmerman prior to an arrest warrant being issued, he or she could have been criminally prosecuted for kidnapping or illegally detaining Zimmerman. In what appeared to be a political move, the Florida State Attorney's office took over the local police department's investigation of the Martin shooting, apparently in reaction to the public outcry.

Zimmerman claimed Trayvon attacked him, broke his nose, and banged his head onto concrete, and that's why he shot Trayvon—he feared for his life. A facial photo taken after the altercation showed Zimmerman with a bloody nose and mouth. A subsequent medical examination confirmed Zimmerman's broken nose, lacerations on the back of his head, two black eyes, and a back injury. Trayvon's autopsy revealed that his knuckles were injured and there were trace amounts of marijuana in his blood. The injured knuckles appear to corroborate Zimmerman's story; however, it could also indicate Trayvon was defending himself from Zimmerman. Other than the bullet wound and injured knuckles, there were no other injuries on Trayvon's body.

Zimmerman was also accused of racial profiling because Trayvon was black, an accusation supposedly supported by comments

Zimmerman made to 911. NBC's *Today Show* ran an edited audio of Zimmerman's 911 call in which he appears to say, "This guy looks like he's up to no good. He looks black" (FoxNews.com 2012).

This would indicate racial profiling by Zimmerman, but the audio recording in its entirety revealed that Zimmerman did not volunteer the information that Trayvon was black. Instead, Zimmerman was answering a question, from the 911 operator, about Trayvon's race (FoxNews.com 2012). Zimmerman said, "This guy looks like he's up to no good. Or he's on drugs or something. It's raining, and he's just walking around, looking about." The 911 operator responded, "Okay, and this guy—is he black, white, or Hispanic?" Zimmerman answered, "He looks black."

Even though NBC apologized for the misleading editing, Zimmerman filed a civil suit against NBC for defamation of character and slander.

The local police department was accused of a cover-up for failing to initially arrest Zimmerman and conducting an inadequate investigation. These allegations were later refuted by a Florida State Attorney who praised the investigative work of the local police department even though, as a direct consequence of these allegations, the white police chief was fired by the black city manager. The news media was complicit in adding credibility to these pretrial allegations, thus furthering the presumption of Zimmerman's guilt and rush to judgment. As it turned out, the State Attorney's office initially decided there was not enough evidence to support an arrest. The police were instructed to release Zimmerman subject to an investigation by the State Attorney's office that later resulted in Zimmerman's arrest and being charged with second-degree murder.

As a result of news media-enabled rushes to judgment, outcries of moral indignation, accusations of racism, and death threats, Zimmerman has been forced to remain in hiding. On the one-year anniversary of Zimmerman's arrest, his mother penned an open letter defending her son. The below extract summarized my concerns:

> The media, with the help of social media, made it their prerogative to judge and sentence George before and after his arrest. Even members of Congress and self-proclaimed "activists" used and routinely use to this day the term "murderer" when they speak of him—in effect they are re-enforcing the only acceptable judicial outcome in their

eyes. Many have seen to it that he be judged by the public, the very public they were keen on misinforming. (Huffington Post 2013)

In July 2013, Zimmerman's trial ended with a not-guilty verdict; however, since before the trial, Zimmerman has been demonized and become a lightning rod for the polarizing debates about the Stand Your Ground law, unequal justice, and racism in America.

There are many questions regarding what really happened that tragic night, which again is the reason for presuming innocence until proven guilty. Now that the trial is over, in addition to respecting the verdict, I hope Americans and the news media reflect on what appears to be an increasing propensity to rush to judgment and presume guilt rather than innocence, especially in high-profile cases. In judicial parlance, justice is a process, not a result. The presumption of innocence is part of this process and is supposed to apply to *all* Americans—including Zimmerman. To all who presumed George Zimmerman to be guilty before his trial—*Is he only an American when the mood suits you?*

Paying for an Attorney

If someone is arrested and can afford an attorney, why does he or she have to pay for one, and if the case is dismissed with prejudice (double jeopardy is attached) or results in an acquittal, why can't the defendant be reimbursed for his or her legal fees?

To the first half of the question, Americans have the unalienable right to the pursuit of happiness, and in order to do this, being financially viable is a necessity. If the government impedes the ability to exercise this right, such as when someone is arrested and incarcerated, the burden of payment should always fall on the government regardless of the accused's ability to pay. The accused would still have the option to refuse a free court-appointed attorney, and retain and pay for an attorney of choice. As occurs with exorbitant medical fees, there are many examples where defendants are left with crippling legal fees after a criminal trial, sometimes resulting in bankruptcy. In my opinion, this is not what the Framers of the Constitution intended. The Sixth Amendment states that "in all criminal prosecutions, the accused shall enjoy the right to . . . have the assistance of counsel for his defense" (Legal Information Institute).

Nowhere does it speak to a distinction between the ability and lack of ability to *afford* counsel. In my opinion, if the state makes the arrest, the state should pay for the rest. However, states can use the opposing argument that the Sixth Amendment only mandates the right to counsel and does not dictate how counsel is to be provided or paid for, thus rendering the Sixth Amendment ambiguous at best. Since the ambiguity of the Sixth Amendment allows for two different interpretations, it is convenient for states to choose the latter opinion, thus allowing the argument that they do not have the funding to support free court-appointed attorneys for everyone. In other words, states take the cheapest route; in order to obtain a free court-appointed attorney, the accused would have to convince a judge that he or she cannot afford to hire one.

The only way to be reimbursed for legal fees is to sue in civil court for reimbursement and damages if malfeasance, such as prosecutorial misconduct, malicious prosecution, or false arrest, occurred—and reimbursement is not guaranteed. As in gambling, if a bet is lost, the gambler pays, and if the gambler wins, he or she gets paid. The police gamble that the accused is the guilty party. The prosecution gambles it can prove that the defendant is guilty. They both hedge their bets by involuntarily detaining an accused person and, in lieu of incarceration, requiring bail to ensure the accused's presence in court, thus impeding the accused's rights to liberty and the pursuit of happiness. If the authorities lose the bet via an acquittal or case dismissal, the defendant still pays the total cost of his or her defense, with the exception of reimbursed bail and, only in the state of Florida, reimbursement of court-related costs such as expert witness testimony, subpoenas, process servers, and court reporter fees.

Blackmail is threatening to reveal embarrassing, disgraceful, or damaging information about a person to the public, family, spouse, or associates unless money is paid to purchase silence—a form of extortion. Because the information is usually substantially true, it is not revealing the information that is a crime, but demanding money to withhold it (US Legal).

If defendants can afford an attorney, the state is basically stating that defendants must pay for an attorney in order to defend themselves against public accusations that are embarrassing, disgraceful, or damaging. Granted, the prosecution revealing the accusations is not a crime. Requiring defendants to *pay* for an attorney to defend against the accusations is the crime. Under cover of official authority, the prosecution is threatening a defendant, resulting in the loss of money to an attorney, all of which could be considered legalized blackmail. Again, if the defendant is acquitted or the case is dismissed, the state should be penalized in the form of reimbursing legal fees for losing the case and failing to justify the impediments on a defendant's constitutional rights. Also, by providing free court-appointed attorneys to only those who cannot pay, is this in effect unconstitutional discrimination against everyone who can afford an attorney?

I know my approach would fundamentally change major components of the judicial process, but an American citizen should not have to pay for the constitutionally mandated right to counsel unless he or she chooses to do so. If one of the core functions of government is to ensure a judicial process based on the equitable protection of constitutionally mandated rights, then it is fair to argue that the government providing free counsel to all in criminal prosecutions, regardless of a defendant's ability to afford counsel, should be a mandatory part of that process.

Right to Privacy

As far as I am concerned, the news media constantly and with impunity violates an individual's rights to privacy for the sake of a scoop, under the guise of the public's right to know and the protection of the First Amendment. The Constitution contains no expressed right to privacy; however, the Bill of Rights addresses aspects of privacy, such as the privacy of beliefs, our homes against demands that it be used to house soldiers, our person and possessions against unreasonable searches and seizures, and self-incrimination to include the privacy of personal information (Linder, The Right To Privacy). Violators of these rights could be subject to civil court action. Herein is a possible solution to news media's intrusions into an individual's privacy.

Since a New York prosecutor successfully sued Tawana Brawley and her advisors, why not sue the news media? The news media was just as culpable for being the instrument that widely communicated character assassinations and related diatribe on both sides of the Brawley argument. Due to its overwhelming power and influence, the news media should be held to a very high standard. Based on the presumption of innocence until proven guilty, and prior to a verdict in a court of law, our right to privacy should include legal protection for the accused and accusers against the news media's intrusiveness and resulting defamation of character. In this regard, one would think the media would be held legally accountable for this type of behavior—not necessarily. In the 1967 US Supreme Court case *Time, Inc. v. Hill,* Justice Brennan wrote the majority opinion that reversed a previous ruling in favor of Hill, who was suing *Time Magazine* for printing false information:

> The majority opinion held that states cannot judge in favor of plaintiffs to redress false reports of matters of public interest in the absence of proof that the defendant published the report with knowledge of its falsity or reckless disregard of the truth. (*Time, Inc. v. Hill*)

What if the actual truth is not known and the news media communicates unsubstantiated supposition and allegations, resulting in an implied and premature message of guilt prior to a court verdict? Even when the truth is not known, such actions should be considered a willful and reckless disregard of an individual's right to privacy and presumption of innocence. Violators should be held criminally or civilly liable, as appropriate. This approach would give the news media and television commentators pause, making them think before they speak.

Below are other ideas to ensure the constitutional presumption of innocence and right to privacy. Ideally, these ideas would have the strength of federal law that compels all states to comply:

- Disallow the public communication of an accused's name, image, and other personal information unless the accused is convicted in a court of law or enters into a plea bargain to avoid a harsher punishment. If the accused is not arrested or convicted, continue to disallow dissemination unless approved by the accused.
- Do not allow live public television or audio coverage of criminal or civil trials, to include recordings, cameras, and sketch artists. Allow the court to videotape trials, archive the videotape as

public record, and make it accessible to the media and public after the trial is completed. If for any reason the defendant is acquitted or wins the civil case, disallow dissemination unless approved by the defendant.

- Enjoin, via a gag order, all persons attending a trial to abide by the above conditions or be held in contempt of court.
- If anyone not attending a trial obtains the defendant's personal information and communicates this information contrary to the above restrictions, arrest the violator. If such information is communicated by the news media, violators can additionally be legally compelled to reveal their sources as an exception to shield laws and be sued in civil court.

In 2013, Cook County, Illinois, courthouses mirrored several of these recommendations by banning electronic devices, such as cell phones, smartphones, tablets, laptops, and all other electronic devices capable of connecting to the Internet or making audio or video recordings. This ban was enacted to prevent the improper communication of testimony to witnesses waiting to testify and to protect witnesses from having their testimony illegally recorded or pictures taken, thus exposing them to potential witness intimidation, physical harm, or murder (Huffington Post 2013).

As stated earlier, the Constitution does not contain an expressed right to privacy—it is implied. However, I believe that protecting a citizen's privacy far outweighs the news media's and public's right to know. The news media obviously does not agree.

"The Jury Will Disregard . . ."

If a tree falls in a forest and no one is around to hear it, does it make a sound?

How many times has a judge instructed a jury to disregard inappropriate testimony, questions, or comments from attorneys, witnesses, or the accused? It is a common practice for defense or prosecuting attorneys to "poison the well" by intentionally asking an inappropriate question or making a statement they know will be thrown out by the judge, but heard by the jury regardless. Conscientious jurors will make honest efforts to disregard what should not have been heard, but what are the subconscious impacts on the juror's decision making during jury deliberations? The mind consciously or subconsciously processes all it hears and forgets little. When a tree falls in court, it definitely makes a sound.

One way for a jury to disregard such statements is to ensure they never hear them in the first place. Why not place the jury in a separate room with a time-delayed video feed? If the judge strikes certain testimony, edit it from the video feed, and the jury will never hear it. The court could view the jury through a video feed into the court room. If an unruly defendant can be removed from the courtroom and allowed to observe the proceedings from a separate room with a real-time video feed, without violating his or her constitutional rights, why not do the same for a jury with a time-delayed video feed?

To prevent concerns as to the accuracy or authenticity of the jury's video feed, a real-time, unedited video could be made that includes everything that occurred during the trial—all corroborated by the trial transcript that is prepared by the court recorder. Lastly, to ensure the proper conduct of the jury watching the video feed, a Special Master could sit with the jury while court is in session, and a silent widescreen television positioned where the jury would normally sit in the courtroom so the court could also observe the jury except during deliberations.

In conclusion, if a tree falls in court and the jury does not hear it, it will not make a sound.

Tort Reform

Tort is a negligent or intentional civil wrong not arising out of a contract or statute. This includes intentional torts, such as battery, defamation, and negligence. A tort is an act that injures someone, for which the injured person may sue the wrongdoer for damages in civil court. Legally, torts are called civil wrongs as opposed to criminal wrongs. Acts such as battery may be both torts and crimes, with the wrongdoer facing both civil and criminal penalties (The 'Lectric Law Library). For example, OJ Simpson was criminally charged with murder, acquitted, and then successfully sued in civil court for wrongful death.

Currently, there is a debate about the need for tort reform to minimize the economic impacts of massive civil damage awards. A more graphic opinion regarding this issue is that "greed has turned the temple of justice, long a hallowed place, into a pigsty . . . Like a plague of locusts, US lawyers with their clients have descended upon America and are suing the country out of business" (Edith Greene).

Whether or not Americans are overly litigious is a question for another time, but what is not in question is the existence of extraordinarily high civil awards. As solutions to curb excessive civil awards, there are proposals to place caps on punitive and noneconomic damage awards and establish equitable benchmarks to determine the amount of compensatory damages to award for wrongful loss, injury, or death. I agree with both proposals because America is in dire need of tort reform.

There are two types of civil damage awards—compensatory and punitive. Compensatory damages (actual and quantifiable damages, plus pain and suffering) are awarded to compensate for loss, injury, or harm suffered as a result of another's actions or breach of duty. Punitive damages are awarded in order to reform or deter a defendant and others from pursuing a similar course of action in the future, and only in cases where the defendant's conduct was significantly egregious, such as in the case of malicious intent. The awarded amount is in addition to awarded compensatory damages ("Damages").

Property damage, where the replacement value is a known market price, is easy to quantify—but it is difficult to quantify injuries to one's body or mind. What is the monetary value civil law assigns to our person or our mental or emotional capacities if we are wrongfully injured or die? Since there is no market value for a lost leg or someone's sanity, there is no established price that a court can apply in awarding damages. Some courts have developed damage award benchmarks that relate to the severity of an injury. For example, in the United Kingdom, the loss or fracture of a thumb is compensated up to £18,000 ($28,500), an arm up to £72,000 ($114,226), two arms up to £150,000 ($237,965), and so on (100% Compensation). But this is not the case in the United States.

> There is no scientific formula and no chart or table juries, attorneys or insurance companies can look to. . . . Two people can have the same injury and one can suffer little while the

> other suffers a great deal; or one offers better proof than the
> other with more complete documentation or better witnesses;
> or they can be in two different parts of the country and get
> completely different settlements or awards. (Free Advice)

Civil courts constantly struggle with the question of value while awarding punitive damages that can be millions or billions of dollars. For example, as of mid-2013, the largest civil damage award on record is a personal injury award of $150 billion against one individual. Some argue that extraordinary punitive damage awards are the result of the jury system.

> Jurors bring their experiences with them into the jury room
> and are sometimes influenced by their preexisting notions
> of justice and equity. They are sometimes impermissibly
> influenced by race and wealth, and they are often confused
> about the law. (Bornstein 2003)

Fortunately, a vindictive or malicious jury award can be lowered or reversed by a higher court. For example, a Florida civil verdict of $145 billion against the tobacco industry was later overturned on appeal (MSNBC.com 2011).

Another factor increasing punitive damage awards is the agreement between lawyers and clients in which a share of the awarded damages is given as payment to the attorney, thus giving the attorney an economic incentive for high punitive awards. This payment is usually 33 percent of the awarded damages. Such agreements, while legal in the US, are considered unethical in the European Union ("Tort Reform").

The resulting effect of civil mega awards is astronomical malpractice insurance premiums for doctors and similar professions, plus higher prices for goods and services provided by corporations and other businesses—resulting in a crushing economic burden when the costs are passed on to the consumer and the economy as a whole. In the medical profession, a consequence is that many doctors are leaving high-risk medical specialties such as obstetrics, resulting in reduced availability of quality health care in these areas. Another consequence is that many doctors practice defensive medicine, ordering unnecessary tests and procedures for fear of malpractice suits and thereby increasing health care costs.

How can these issues be resolved? Again, I believe tort reform is necessary and should include these considerations:

- I believe it is within the intent of the Constitution to allow for and mandate equitable federal standards and limits in the determination of civil damage awards—standards and limits all states would be compelled to follow. As in current law, states would still be able to apply lower, but not higher, standards. Consider these suggestions:
  - o Continue the current practice of placing no limits on damage awards for quantifiable economic damages.
  - o As some states have already established, establish a range and hard cap on damage awards for pain and suffering (such as \$50,000–\$300,000 per occurrence) and wrongful death (such as \$250,000–\$500,000 per occurrence). Both should only be adjusted for inflation.
  - o In the same manner as the UK, establish a table of bodily and mental injuries with a damage award range and hard cap for each injury—adjusted only for inflation.
  - o Regarding punitive awards, establish a hard cap multiplier of compensatory damages awarded, such as three times per occurrence of nonbodily harm damages, five times per occurrence of bodily or mental harm, or seven times per occurrence of wrongful death. There is precedent for this. For example, treble compensatory damages can be awarded for willful violation of antitrust laws, patent infringement, trademark counterfeiting, and violations under the RICO statute ("Trebel Damages").
  - o When an attorney accepts a civil case on contingency, as allowable compensation, place a hard cap maximum percentage of the total of compensatory and punitive damages awarded. For federal cases, a maximum cap of 20 to 25 percent is mandated depending on the type of case.

- Establishing federally mandated hard caps and ranges would serve two purposes:

o Provide consistency and remove the excessive and arbitrary nature of determining civil damage awards. This also allows defendants and insurance companies to know, with a reasonable degree of certainty, what to expect if a defendant is found liable. Risk could be more accurately quantified and, with restrictions on excessive awards, insurance premiums would be significantly lowered.

o There would be significant economic benefits, such as the lowering of health care costs, and increases in the availability of health care and other goods and services.

The Declaration of Independence states that all men (and women) are created equal. The monetary value placed on a life, body, and mind should also be equal, with legal exceptions noted in determining compensatory lost wages or future earnings due to an injury or death. There is a common belief that the value of a human life is intrinsically priceless, and since a plaintiff cannot be awarded infinite damages, tort reform is a logical approach to stem the draining economic impacts of out-of-control damage awards.

Torture and Indefinite Detention

A prisoner should not be incarcerated indefinitely without due process of law or tortured. In opposition to torture, W. C. Green wrote on the website DemocraticUnderground.com:

> A while back I wrote a thread about how the US was an exceptional nation. It is because we are a nation held together only by our belief in the rule of law. How this [torture] will play out will determined [sic] if we are indeed unique or just another in a long string of tin horned empires. (Green 2009)

How indefinite detention and torture play out will determine if America truly believes in the rule of law or turns a blind eye when it is convenient.

In 2009, President Obama issued Executive Order 13491 that requires the CIA and other federal executive agencies to use the nineteen interrogation techniques outlined in Army Field Manual 2-22.3, *Human Intelligence Collector Operations* (Department of the Army 2006). The nineteen methods focus on benign techniques, not torture, to help establish a rapport with a prisoner and elicit truthful answers to questions (President Barack Obama 2009). Even though my concerns about torture were hopefully eliminated by President Obama, vigilance will be necessary to ensure that torture remains a memory. Everyone in America should watch the 2013 TV documentary *Standard Operating Procedures*, which examined the Abu Ghraib prison atrocities—death, beatings, waterboarding, and the deplorable sexual humiliation of Iraqi prisoners by US soldiers and intelligence personnel (ENCORE Drama 2013). This documentary would remove all doubt about eliminating torture, also called "enhanced interrogation techniques," as a standard operating procedure in interrogations. Also, let's not forget when America condemned, with profuse moral indignation, the torture of American POWs by North Vietnamese captors during the Vietnam War.

Having said this, there have been debates about the appropriateness of torture in extraordinary circumstances. A classic hypothetical example is the appropriateness of using torture to get information from a prisoner in order to save millions of lives from an imminent terrorist-initiated nuclear explosion. Do the rights of the many outweigh the rights of the few or the one? I must admit that under such extraordinary circumstances, torture may be appropriate. I am acutely aware of the moral dilemma and hypocrisy of decrying torture on one hand while approving its use under extraordinary circumstances; however, I could live with the conflict as long as America does not start sliding down a slippery slope by conveniently expanding the criteria.

Regarding indefinite detention without due process of law, I have no such moral conflicts—it is wrong under *all* circumstances. President Obama needs to end the indefinite detention of prisoners at the Guantanamo Bay Detention Center. Contrary to his stated beliefs, in 2011, President Obama issued Executive Order 13567 that permits the indefinite detention of illegal combatants while establishing a periodic administrative review process for them. He later signed a defense bill with similar provisions that included the possibility of incarcerating American illegal combatants at Guantanamo and detaining them indefinitely (President Barack Obama 2011). However, in 2012, President Obama waived sections of the new detention law that included

American citizens. The section mandating indefinite military detention for all other detainees was overturned by a federal judge and is being appealed by federal prosecutors.

Indefinite detention is an indictment against our system of justice when measured against constitutionally mandated human rights. Where is it written in the Constitution that it is permissible to indefinitely detain an individual without due process of law? (The noted exception is POW/Geneva Convention situations, where detention is allowed until hostilities end which, by definition, is not indefinite.) Did America suspend *habeas corpus* and rewrite the speedy trial clause of the Sixth Amendment by extending the time limit to eight years (the longest time, as of 2012, a detainee has been detained at Guantanamo without a trial)? And herein is the problem. America's human rights track record is not pristine regarding illegal or inappropriate detention. The most obvious examples are slavery and the forced relocation of Native Americans and Japanese Americans to federal reservations and internment camps, respectively. Is America's history repeating itself with the indefinite detention of known or suspected terrorists?

No president should have the power to declare the entire world a war zone without a formal declaration of war and then detain prisoners anywhere on the globe, holding them indefinitely without due process of law. The Bush and Obama administrations did exactly that by claiming the authority to detain, without charge or trial, prisoners who they deem engaged in the war on terror (ACLU). A combatant's classification (terrorist or illegal combatant) should not be the standard by which the applied level of justice is determined. It is supposed to be equal justice for all, and if America continues down this path, what would this say about the rule of law? For "nothing destroys the credibility of a government faster than its failure to provide fair and equal justice for its people" (Skousen 1986).

If America wants to be the role model for democracy throughout the world, providing fair and equitable justice should apply to all people— not just American citizens. Hopefully, torture has been eliminated as a standard operating procedure. In the same vein, indefinite detention is contrary to basic human and civil rights, should be declared unconstitutional, and should be eliminated.

On an encouraging closing note, during an address on May 23, 2013, President Obama recommitted to close Guantanamo by asking Congress to lift restrictions preventing such an action and to process all prisoners either through selective repatriation to other countries, or through relocation to America and eventual adjudication via due process of law. Time will tell if his words are translated into action.

US Supreme Court Appointments

Since Supreme Court justices are appointed for life, I propose a law that requires a 4/4/1 composition of four conservative and four liberal associate justices with a chief justice that must be a moderate. If not 4/4/1, mandate term limits. The possibility of a politically skewed Supreme Court combined with lifetime appointments of Supreme Court justices concerns me. Lower-court federal judges also serve for life, and my concerns also apply to them; however, this discussion will be limited to the highest judicial authority in America—the Supreme Court.

The Supreme Court's job performance approval level was 80 percent in 1994. However, according to a recent poll conducted in 2012, only 44 percent of Americans approved of the Supreme Court's performance, with a majority believing the justices decide cases based on their personal or political views rather than along constitutional lines. Additionally, 60 percent agreed that appointing Supreme Court justices for life was not good because it gave them too much power. Only one-third said that lifetime appointments were appropriate (Huffington Post 2012).

4/4/1

Mandate four conservative and four liberal associate justices with a chief justice that must be a moderate.

Expressing the ultimate responsibility of the court, "Equal Justice Under Law" is inscribed above the main entrance to the Supreme Court Building. The US Supreme Court is the highest tribunal in the nation and, as the final arbiter of the law, is charged with ensuring equal justice under law and also functions as the guardian and interpreter of the Constitution. The Supreme Court does not give advisory opinions or create policy or law. The Constitution limits the court to cases and controversies arising under the Constitution or laws of the United States (Linder, *The Supreme Court in the American System of Government* 2012).

Supreme Court justices are appointed by the president of the United States, are confirmed by the Senate, serve for life, and can only be removed if they are impeached and removed from office for misconduct or leave by resigning, retiring, or dying. As of June 2013, the Supreme Court's membership and judicial inclinations are as follows:

- **Conservative**: Alito, Roberts (chief justice), Scalia, and Thomas—appointed by Republican presidents.
- **Moderate**: Kennedy (the swing vote)—appointed by a Republican president.
- **Liberal**: Breyer, Ginsburg, Kagan, and Sotomayor—appointed by Democratic presidents.

This court's ideological composition is evenly matched with one moderate as a swing vote (tie-breaker); however, this composition is by chance and not by design or mandate, and that is worrisome.

In a democracy, the majority usually rules—a simple majority of 51 percent or higher. There are exceptions to this rule, such as needing a 60 percent majority in the Senate to stop a filibuster, and in corporate America where a supermajority of 80 percent is needed to pass certain shareholder resolutions. The Supreme Court makes rulings based on a simple majority of five votes out of nine, and if a justice is sick, recuses himself or herself, or is otherwise unavailable, resulting in a 4/4 tie, a tie vote upholds the ruling of the lower court.

This is all well and good, but what if the court's composition is a majority or 100 percent conservative or liberal? The Warren Court is an excellent example. It was 100 percent liberal, and all the justices were appointed by liberal presidents Franklin D. Roosevelt and Harry Truman. Under these circumstances, would the court's skewed composition result in rulings that reflect the prevailing political climate at the time? Granted, the Warren Court reflected America's liberal tendencies during its tenure, but the opposite could very easily be the case under the current appointment system.

Of all presidential elections, President Lyndon Johnson captured the highest popular vote percentage (61 percent) in 1964; however, only 62 percent of voting-age citizens actually voted. Doing the math, President Johnson only captured approximately 38 percent of the vote of all American citizens of voter age—far short of a simple majority. Also, for the sake of argument, let's assume that this dynamic also applies to our elected congressional leaders. In short, congressional leaders are elected that do not reflect the true majority of the constituency they are elected to represent (InfoPlease 2011). Therefore, it is also possible to appoint a politically skewed court that does not represent the ideological demographics or inclinations of the American constituency.

Let's not forget that US Supreme Court rulings affect *all* citizens— not just voters. This is why I propose a law that mandates four conservative and four liberal associate justices with a chief justice that must be a moderate. Regardless of who is the president or has a congressional majority, all sides of the political and judicial spectrum would be equitably represented in the court's rulings. If 4/4/1 was mandated, I would be comfortable with lifetime appointments.

The president of the United States is limited to two consecutive four-year terms and must win reelection to serve a second term. Senators serve for a six-year term and must win reelection for additional terms. Those elected to the House of Representatives serve a two-year term and must win reelection for additional terms. Granted, if congressional leadership wins all their elections, they can in effect serve for life. However, I am okay with this because term limits require elections that give Americans an opportunity to reaffirm or change the political ideology that will guide legislative actions. With lifetime appointments, no such opportunity exists with the Supreme Court.

Term Limits

Before discussing term limits, it is important to understand the historical context and rationale behind appointing Supreme Court justices and federal judges for life.

In the eighteenth century, part of the debate involved the power of the king or queen to remove and appoint judges at will. Liberals believed that lifetime appointments would scale back the power of the monarchy and ensure social progress. If a judge was appointed for life, he could vote according to his own judicial judgment despite the wishes or influence of the ruling monarchy. The writers of the Constitution saw lifetime appointments in the same light, as a way to limit the strength and influence of the executive branch of government ("Why are US Supreme Court justices appointed for life?").

Without 4/4/1 or term limits, my concern is that lifetime appointments do not actually limit executive strength—they perpetuate it. A lifetime appointment ensures a lifetime of judicial influence based on the political ideology of the appointing and confirming entities and not necessarily the prevailing ideology of the population over time. Another obvious concern is that judges may, due to advancing age, become less capable of appropriately analyzing legal arguments in order to develop cogent and well-thought-out legal opinions. Without 4/4/1, term limits would eliminate these concerns.

Appoint Supreme Court justices for an eight-year term and require Senate reconfirmation at the end of every term. If confirmed, a justice would serve for another eight-year term. If not confirmed, the president and Senate would have to appoint and confirm another justice. Stagger reconfirmations to prevent a 100 percent turnover of the court at the same time. Term limits would serve two purposes:

- The possibility of a permanent and politically skewed court would be negated because the court's judicial inclinations would be more synchronized with the prevailing ideologies of the population.
- Every justice would have to demonstrate that they are still physically, mentally, and emotionally capable of performing their duties.

US Supreme Court justices serve we the people. Americans need to ensure they are always in tune with who we are.

Chapter 3

POLITICS

Are we only to be Americans when the mood suits you?

Recent polls indicate an alarming lack of trust and confidence in the leaders charged with America's governance and representation, specifically lawmakers in Congress. The divisiveness in government and political infighting leaves one to wonder if we the people are just pawns in a political chess match to be nurtured as Americans only during elections. Are elected officials representing Americans' interests or their own? To answer these questions, I will focus on five topics:

- Election-Year Politics
- Politicizing National Tragedies
- Politics, Racism, or Both
- Three-Party Political System
- Voter Intimidation by Employers

Election-Year Politics

Election-year politics have become tragic comedies—the height of equivocation regarding politicians' true positions on the issues, and shameless pandering to solicit constituent votes coupled with continual attacks on political opponents' character and broken promises. What is needed is a complete paradigm shift regarding political integrity and representation—a shift from self-interest and political survival to the interests of we the people. To provide the appropriate context, let's look at a few iconic political speeches by actual and fictional presidents that suggested or initiated such a shift.

There have been several classic political speeches in the last two centuries, such as President Lincoln's Gettysburg Address, President

Kennedy's "Ask not what your country can do for you" inaugural speech, and President Lyndon Johnson's "We Shall Overcome" civil rights speech before a joint session of Congress that resulted in paradigm shifts in America's ethos and social mores. However, there is one speech that I would characterize as one of the best political speeches of all time, delivered by a fictitious Democratic president, Andrew Shepherd, in the 1995 movie *The American President*. Shepherd's comments suggest a much-needed paradigm shift in election campaigning and governance.

In the movie, it is a presidential election year and fictional Senator Bob Rumson is President Shepherd's Republican opponent. While campaigning, Rumson continually attacks Shepherd's character. Shepherd refuses to respond to Rumson's attacks until he has an epiphany resulting in one of the most impactful political speeches I have ever heard. During a White House press conference, he responds to Rumson's attacks while maintaining his pledge not to engage in the character assassination game. To summarize his comments, Shepherd wrote crime prevention legislation that pandered to the gun lobby by omitting restrictions on the use of handguns and assault rifles. He reversed himself by withdrawing the original legislation to rewrite it in what he believed were in the best interests of the American people instead of his own reelection interests. While questioning Rumson's leadership qualifications and understanding of the Bill of Rights, he unambiguously states his position on various issues, such as his ACLU membership. Shepherd also admits that up until the time of his epiphany, he had been so busy trying to keep his job, he forgot to do his job—a common occurrence among too many politicians and an excellent segue to a discussion about dubious election-year politics such as broken promises, character assassination, flip-flopping, and pandering.

Broken Promises

Politicians should not make promises they are not sure they can keep. What politicians want to happen versus what they are able to make happen are all too often two very different realities. Sometimes politicians believe they can dangle promised carrots in front of constituents' faces, and that constituents will continue pulling the politicians' carts like gullible mules. Irritate a mule and you'll get a painful kick from its hind legs or, in my case, my vote. President George H. W. Bush learned this lesson when, during the 1988 Republican National Convention, he made the infamous "read my lips—no new taxes" promise; when he was elected president, he had to raise taxes. Even though the tax increase was necessary, it was not the act of raising taxes that hurt Bush in his reelection bid—it was the breaking of a promise.

President Obama learned a similar lesson. During his 2008 presidential campaign, he promised the public option in health care legislation, yet as president he compromised on a package that did not include the public option. He promised to close the Guantanamo Bay Detention Center, and after one term in office it is still operating. He also promised to address illegal immigration as a priority on his agenda, yet with the exception of an executive order prohibiting the deportation of undocumented minors, comprehensive immigration reform is still on the drawing board.

The issue was not that promises were disingenuously delivered. Presidents George H. W. Bush and Obama sincerely believed they could deliver on their promises, but they became president, and the realities of the office and prevailing socioeconomic and political dynamics brought them both back down to earth. However, voters do not forget broken promises, and if promises continue to go unfulfilled, *read my lips—no new term of office.*

Character Assassination

Character assassination involves rumor mongering, innuendo, and misinformation regarding someone's character or reputation. It may involve sharing information that is technically true, but presented in a misleading manner or without the proper context. As a hypothetical example, a political ad states that an opposing candidate was arrested for assault. The arrest was technically accurate, but the ad conveniently omitted the fact that the charges were dismissed when evidence proved it was justifiable self-defense and not criminal assault.

Character assassination has historically been part of our political processes. Senator Joseph McCarthy destroyed lives and careers in his misguided quest to root out communists in the 1950s. President Nixon was accused of a variety of impeachable crimes in his attempts to destroy the credibility and character of political opponents. President Obama was called a liar, and his citizenship was challenged. Lastly, the presidential campaign of 1828 has been characterized as one of the dirtiest of all time, rife with false accusations, character attacks, and innuendo between John Quincy Adams and Andrew Jackson (McNamara, The Election of 1828 Was Marked By Dirty Tactics).

Contemporary politicians should be elated that defamation-of-character issues are resolved in court and not in the manner that existed in eighteenth- and nineteenth-century America—dueling with pistols, swords, or knives. The most notable duel was between former Secretary of the Treasury Alexander Hamilton and Vice President Aaron Burr in 1804. Hamilton defamed Burr's character, and the matter was settled the old-fashioned way—with Hamilton dying in a pistol duel. Facetiously speaking, dueling could be a novel solution that prompts more civil and respectful political discourse; however, that was then, and this is now.

When a politician resorts to character assassinations, I suspect the politician of being weak on the real issues and question his or her character. However, even political candidates that appear to be above character assassinations are prone to mistakes. Of note, during the 2012 presidential election campaign, a PAC supportive of President Obama put out a television advertisement against Mitt Romney that stated if Romney had been president, he would not have made the high-risk command decision to go into Pakistan to kill or capture Osama bin Laden—suggesting that Romney would be indecisive as a commander in chief. For this PAC to make such a disparaging statement was very disappointing.

During the same campaign, Republican Representative Michelle Bachmann accused certain members of President Obama's administration of being Muslim Brotherhood infiltrators due to their family or social connections to others with a possible Muslim Brotherhood connection. This is similar to the accusation former Republican Representative Allen West made that there were approximately eighty congressional Democrats who were communists—eerily reminiscent of McCarthyism. Regarding Bachmann's accusation, how many white members of Congress have relatives or friends of relatives who were KKK or other segregationist group members? Does this automatically make them racists? Bachmann spent a summer working on an Israeli kibbutz. Does this make her an

Israeli spy? In apparent attempts to maintain newsworthy and political relevance, Bachmann, West, and others like them make a mockery of political discourse—all under the protection of the First Amendment. They also do an injustice to others who present their ideas or concerns in cogent and respectful manners.

Character assassination is still a very potent political weapon that influences voters and deflects debate from the real issues that need to be addressed. Hopefully, politicians will learn to respect others as they would like to be respected, and focus on the issues. Always remember—attack another person's character, and your own character comes into play.

Flip-Flopping

Altering of personal beliefs happens to all of us throughout our lives; these occurrences are most commonly known in the political arena as "flip-flopping," especially when core beliefs are reversed. Flip-flopping can be a natural and evolutionary process resulting in adjustments of beliefs due to changing social parameters, individual life experiences, or epiphanies, or it can be a disingenuous reversal of stated beliefs to cater to a voting constituency.

Flip-flopping has historically been a debatable part of America's political process, especially during elections. In 1860, President Lincoln promised to preserve the Union rather than ending slavery. Then the Civil War occurred, and Lincoln's Emancipation Proclamation ended slavery. After the 1964 Civil Rights Bill was signed into law, many southern politicians who were staunch segregationists reversed their stated views to a more conciliatory and supportive tone regarding civil rights. Most notably was former Alabama Governor George Wallace's reversal. Wallace stood in the entranceways of segregated Alabama schools to prevent black students from entering to enroll, and he made this infamous declaration during an inaugural address: "In the name of the greatest people that have ever trod this earth, I draw the line in the dust and toss the gauntlet before the feet of tyranny, and I say segregation now, segregation tomorrow, segregation forever" (Pearson 1998).

In the late 1970s, after surviving an assassination attempt and becoming a born-again Christian, Wallace apologized for his past segregationist positions. In his final term as governor, Wallace appointed a record number of blacks to state positions. More recently, politicians such as President Reagan, Senator Joseph Lieberman, and New York City Mayor Michael Bloomberg changed political parties due to dissatisfaction with their former party (Catspirit 2012). President Obama was ambivalent to or totally against same-sex marriage, but after soul-searching and analyzing his presidential responsibilities, he now supports it.

As previously noted, flip-flopping can have a beneficial and progressive effect on politics and governance. However, my greatest concern is with its dark side—politicians espousing the flavor of the day by frequently reversing stated beliefs in order to get elected. This form of flip-flopping raises serious questions about the integrity of a politician's stated positions on the issues as compared to his or her true personal convictions, and what a politician will actually do if elected. Mitt Romney immediately comes to mind. Looking back almost two decades, Romney has flip-flopped on approximately fourteen issues throughout his political career. Reflect on these examples (Dougherty 2012):

- While running for senator from Massachusetts in 1994, Romney once stated he was more pro-choice than his opponent—pro-choice advocate Senator Ted Kennedy. Romney maintained this pro-choice position while campaigning to be elected as Governor of Massachusetts in 2002. However, to run for national office as a conservative Republican, he reversed his position and is now pro-life. Senator Kennedy once said that Romney was not pro-choice; he was "multiple choice" on abortion and other issues.
- As the governor of Massachusetts, Romney championed Massachusetts's health care law that was the blueprint for Obamacare, yet he now questions his own law while opposing Obamacare.
- Romney expressed clear support for a ban on assault rifles, yet in an attempt to obtain NRA backing, he now opposes such bans.
- He endorsed embryonic stem cell research and then proposed criminalizing it.
- He once railed against a flat federal income tax and now appears to support it.

- Romney opposes same-sex marriage and civil unions, but he supports domestic partnership benefits. He supports a federal constitutional amendment defining marriage as between a man and a woman, but if elected president, he would not play a formal role in its passage.

As President Obama stated during the 2012 campaign, Romney seemed to suffer from a form of political dementia called "Romnesia"—a very accurate description of Romney's flip-flopping.

Chameleons can change their body color to blend in with the surrounding landscape in order to hide from predators. Romney's politically expedient and chameleon-like stances on so many issues are bothersome. Politicians who change beliefs as often as chameleons change colors will one day forget what color they are supposed to be in order to represent and advocate for the best interests of their constituents. In short, Americans need to be an informed electorate in order to discern the truth from the chameleons—*before voting*.

Pandering

Pandering is the act of expressing personal or political views in accordance with the likes of a group to which one is attempting to appeal. The term is most notably associated with politics. In political pandering, the views politicians are expressing are merely for the purpose of garnering support and votes.

Even though pandering and flip-flopping are close cousins, pandering is different than flip-flopping. Flip-flopping involves the reversal of stated beliefs. While pandering, a politician's stated beliefs may not change, but the manner in which they are presented changes. It is amazing how a politician's rhetoric changes from their normal manner of speaking depending upon the audience he or she is addressing. Sometimes the pandering borders on the ridiculous. While campaigning in southern states, Mitt Romney used the phrase "y'all" and bragged that he had eaten cheesy grits. This is not the most outrageous example of Romney's pandering. He made very troubling comments during a campaign trip to Alabama in March 2012 while pandering to African American voters:

> In fact, I can relate to black people very well indeed. My ancestors once owned slaves, and it is in my lineage to work closely with the black community. However, just because they were freed over a century ago doesn't mean they can now be freeloaders. They need to be told to work hard, and the incentives just aren't there for them anymore. (Wood 2012)

Romney stating that he could relate to African Americans because his ancestors owned slaves was insulting and patronizing. I am praying that this was just another campaign faux pas that reinforced how detached Romney was from the discriminatory realities African Americans face in America today, and not indicative of deep-seated racist inclinations. Romney unknowingly articulated the continual struggle of African Americans trying to obtain an equal right and access to the opportunities of the American Dream without having to endure the insidious roadblocks of racism. If Romney's comments were a sincere attempt to proactively reach out to African Americans, he was totally out of touch regarding racial issues. This is the case with too many elitist and affluent white politicians, as well as elitist and misguided African Americans such as Justice Clarence Thomas and former US Representative Allen West.

After Romney's gaffe, Vice President Joe Biden made an equally egregious gaffe when he told a majority African American audience that Romney and GOP lawmakers would put them "back in chains." Specifically, he said Romney wanted to get rid of the Wall Street regulations President Obama signed into law, and then stated, "Unchain Wall Street. They're going to put y'all back in chains" (Associated Press and the Huffington Post 2012).

There are rare instances where pandering can have a positive outcome. As described earlier, President Lyndon Johnson had a novel way of referring to the Civil Rights Bill when lobbying for support. When he was talking to supporters of the bill or in public, he would refer to the bill as the Civil Rights Bill. When privately lobbying opposing southern politicians to gain their support and votes, he would pander to their racist inclinations by referring to the bill as the "Nigger Bill." The Civil Rights Bill passed, in large part, due to President Johnson's powers of persuasion and pandering.

There are three politicians I respect for delivering consistent and honest political messages: President Obama (Democrat), New Jersey Governor Chris Christie (Republican), and Representative Ron Paul (Libertarian). They stay on point, and what you see is what you get. Regardless of whether or not I agree with their politics and regardless of their actual performance in office, I trust them to honestly present their views and opinions without pandering and, most importantly, to act in what they sincerely believe are the best interests of the constituency they represent—not just their reelection or political self-interests. These traits are supposed to be commonplace among all elected leaders. On this point, New York City Mayor Michael Bloomberg made a very astute observation that "if you look at people, whether in business or government, who haven't had any moral compass, who've just changed to say whatever they thought the popular thing was, in the end they're losers" (Bloomberg).

Solutions

What can be done about these election-year behaviors? Consider these suggestions:

- Americans need to become a more informed electorate. Ignorance of the issues and candidates is no excuse. Take time to research the candidates' websites, listen to their speeches, research their voting records, watch the debates, and attend the town hall meetings to gain an understanding of their positions on the issues before casting your vote.
- Unlike private citizens, public figures like politicians must prove malice in a defamation civil suit. To stop character assassinations, only during elections and as an exception to the public figure rule, allow political candidates to sue for defamation of character without the requirement to prove malice. If defamation is proved, malice should be automatically assumed because the sole purpose of political character assassinations is to maliciously do intentional harm to the opponent's character and reputation. The offended candidate could also ask the court

for injunctive relief through the issuance of a cease and desist order.

- Implement Truth in Campaigning laws to protect voters from false or misleading information during election campaigns. There are currently Truth in Lending and Truth in Advertising laws to protect the consumer from fraudulent or misleading lending and advertising practices, respectively. A Truth in Campaigning law was enacted in the State of Washington in 2005, but it was overturned by their State Supreme Court. The court's opinion read, in part, that "every person must be his own watchman for truth, because the forefathers did not trust any government to separate the true from the false for us" (Chrish 2005).

  How can someone be a watchman or watchwoman if he or she does not know where to look or what to watch for, lacking the wherewithal to independently verify information or even know what he or she is supposed to be verifying? A Truth in Campaigning law would require that the factual truth be told in the same manner as swearing or affirming to tell the truth during legal proceedings.

The right to vote and a fair electoral process are the linchpins and foundation of a democratic society. It is of paramount importance that the election of those charged with America's governance be based on accurate and well-founded information. Since the individual voter has no means by which he or she can independently verify what is being shared by candidates, the intentional deception of the electorate should be considered illegal—subject to civil or criminal penalties. To intentionally mislead the electorate is tantamount to perpetrating a fraud on we the people.

Finally, the clearest message that can be sent to politicians is to vote. Remember that we will get what we vote for, and if we do not vote, we will have to live with what we get.

Politicizing National Tragedies

On September 11, 2012, the US Consulate in Benghazi, Libya, was attacked by terrorists, resulting in the deaths of a US ambassador and three American members of the ambassador's security detail. Later that same evening, Republican presidential candidate Mitt Romney made a very inappropriate comment while criticizing President Obama, in effect politicizing a tragedy when national solidarity was vital by saying, "It's disgraceful that the Obama administration's first response was not to condemn attacks on our diplomatic missions, but to sympathize with those who waged the attacks" (Vasilogambros 2012).

Romney's comment was politically motivated as much as it was inappropriate and ill-timed. In short, politicizing a national tragedy is disgraceful. Several Republicans agreed with my assessment, but many other Republicans defended Romney. Adding fuel to the heated Benghazi debate, Republican Senators Lindsey Graham and John McCain later besmirched UN Ambassador Susan Rice's integrity for appearing on television and sharing what later turned out to be inaccurate information, talking points she was given by the US intelligence community that suggested the Benghazi attack occurred as a public backlash to a video insulting the Islamic prophet Mohammed. Later, more accurate intelligence pointed to a coordinated attack by terrorists, not an enraged Muslim population.

Let's examine this further. Since the 1960s and prior to the Benghazi incident, there have been several attacks against Americans or American assets resulting in the loss of American lives. Omitting deaths arising from US-initiated military action, Presidents Lyndon Johnson, Carter, Reagan, Clinton, and G. W. Bush had to contend with fatal bombings, murders, hijackings, and other related incidents ranging from one to 2,800-plus deaths. To the best of my memory, America's initial response to these incidents was immediate, with bipartisan political solidarity condemning the attacks and a firm national resolve to mete out justice on the perpetrators. In other words, the national priorities were showing American outrage, patriotism, solidarity, and respect for those who lost their lives, not espousing political ideology or conspiracy theories or attacking the president of the United States at the time of the incident—a notion apparently foreign to Romney.

Regarding Senators McCain's and Graham's attack on Ambassador Rice, even though Ambassador Rice presented inaccurate talking points, McCain and Graham hypocritically accused her of intentionally misleading the American people. They conveniently forgot that, as expressed in an op-ed on the website *Politicususa*, "John McCain supported Condoleezza Rice, who misled the public on WMD [weapons of mass destruction], causing thousands to die, but now attacks Susan Rice" (S. Jones 2012).

Coincidentally, Senator Graham also supported Republican Condoleezza Rice. As an aside, the op-ed omitted reference to the United Nations presentation by former Republican Secretary of State Colin Powell when he presented faulty evidence indicating WMDs in Iraq, a presentation Powell later described as a painful blot on his otherwise stellar record of public service. Regarding Condoleezza Rice, Senators McCain and Graham believed that she acted in good faith and, because of faulty intelligence, should not be held accountable or further criticized for her WMD assertions—a measure of understanding and forgiveness they did not extend to Democratic presidential appointee Ambassador Susan Rice. It should also be noted that neither Graham nor McCain called for the resignations of Condoleezza Rice or Colin Powell, yet they vowed to block the nomination of Ambassador Rice to become secretary of state if so nominated by President Obama. Because of the political fervor associated with her Benghazi comments and potential nomination, Ambassador Rice voluntarily withdrew her name from consideration. Criticizing Ambassador Rice and impugning her integrity, for doing *the exact same thing* as Condoleezza Rice and Colin Powell, could be described as unmitigated hypocrisy.

I hope that Senators McCain and Graham were not trying to undermine President Obama's presidency by adding another divisive political dimension to the Benghazi tragedy in a manner similar to someone suffering from Münchausen Syndrome By Proxy (MSBP). MSBP describes behaviors in which a caregiver deliberately exaggerates, fabricates, and induces physical, psychological, behavioral, or mental health problems in those who are in their care ("Münchausen Syndrome By Proxy"). As elected caregivers of their respective constituencies and America's system of governance, are McCain and Graham inducing unnecessary public frustration and alarm by politicizing the Benghazi tragedy in order to advance their own political agendas? Their reactions to Ambassador Rice's comments make me wonder.

Politics, Racism, or Both

During the week of May 12, 2013, after the GOP backlash regarding the Benghazi terrorist attack, President Obama was bombarded with several contentious issues concerning the Associated Press, the Internal Revenue Service coupled with subsequent comparisons to former President Nixon, and another event that was nicknamed "Umbrella-Gate." As I absorbed the reactions to President Obama regarding these recent events, it became increasingly difficult to distinguish genuine race-neutral political disagreement from racist diatribe and manipulation.

If there was criminality on the part of President Obama or anyone in his administration, all involved should be held accountable and prosecuted as appropriate. Since no evidence of criminality was been presented, what is of concern is how President Obama was treated as compared to other presidents in similar situations. Also, with the exception of the Benghazi attack, all of these events came to light within a one-week period—very interesting timing. Was the timing politically engineered or contrived racist maneuvering? Given the nature of the events in question, it is hard to determine the true motivations for the unrelenting criticism; however, a racist component cannot be discounted.

Associated Press

A leak of classified materials involving the AP, according to the Department of Justice (DOJ), put lives in danger and national security at risk. The DOJ issued subpoenas against the AP to identify the source of the leak. This action resulted in a severe backlash directed at President Obama and Attorney General Holder for alleged violations of the First Amendment by the DOJ. I also have questions about the subpoenas; however, in this discussion, my concern is about the consistency of negative reactions.

President G. W. Bush signed the Patriot Act into law in 2001. The Patriot Act, specifically 50 USC section 1861, gave the federal government unprecedented authority to target American citizens' telephone calls (especially international calls) and intrude upon other aspects of individual privacy—in some cases without subpoenas or search warrants. President Bush received partisan pushback from the political left and opposition from the ACLU and similar watchdog groups, but not to the extent of the vitriolic reactions against President Obama and Attorney General Holder for the AP event.

From my perspective, the reduced level of negative reactions to the intrusive components of the Patriot Act could indicate that protecting the rights of the press is more important than protecting the rights of individual American citizens. By my interpretation of the Constitution, the protection should be applied equally, which would lead me to expect an equal level of outrage if either protection was violated. If my interpretation of the Constitution is correct, and given the heightened level of negative reactions to the AP event, this prompts an interesting question. In addition to an obvious political component, is there also a racial component that is fueling the vitriol hurled at President Obama and Attorney General Holder?

It should be noted that in June 2013, the National Security Agency (NSA) came under fire for collecting, under color of the Patriot Act, telephone metadata on American citizens. This is being investigated by Congress.

Benghazi

Even though the Benghazi attack occurred in September 2012, it is worth mentioning in this discussion to further establish context.

President Obama lost *four* Americans, who were killed in Benghazi due to a terrorist attack, and he was subsequently condemned for failing to secure the attacked diplomatic mission and accused of conducting an alleged cover-up. Republican President G. W. Bush ordered the military into Iraq (Operation Iraqi Freedom) based on faulty intelligence that indicated Iraq had WMDs and ties to al-Qaeda, allegations that were proved false. Operation Iraqi Freedom resulted in the deaths of 4,440-plus US service members. President Bush was subjected to harsh and embarrassing questioning when WMDs were not found in Iraq, yet where was the outrage? Where were the demands for him to be held accountable and impeached for what could arguably be classified as 4,440-plus counts of wrongful death?

Additionally, was Republican President Reagan vilified when 241 US Marines were killed in Lebanon when their barracks were bombed due to security deficiencies? Was Democratic President Clinton vilified for Mogadishu, Somalia, where eighteen US Army Rangers were killed and their bodies publically desecrated without retribution on the perpetrators? Was President G. W. Bush vilified for 9/11, when 2,800-plus souls were killed and it was discovered there were intelligence failures, plus a general lack of preparedness and coordination to quickly respond to such domestic airborne scenarios?

With the exception of Somalia and Operation Iraqi Freedom, all the aforementioned deaths were the result of terrorist attacks and, in all cases, the security of the affected facilities and effectiveness of operational policies, procedures, or protocols were questioned, yet the reactions toward the presidents involved paled in comparison to the criticism President Obama endured as a result of Benghazi and the loss of *four* lives. It is also interesting that most of the backlash directed at President Obama was not about the Benghazi deaths, but rather the origin and validity of official talking points that many Republicans felt pointed to an alleged cover-up by the Obama administration.

Internal Revenue Service

The IRS inappropriately targeted the Tea Party and other conservative political groups applying for tax-exempt status. As a consequence, the acting head of the IRS resigned, and the DOJ initiated a criminal probe into the IRS's actions—all appropriate actions. An independent inspector general investigation and sworn congressional testimony clearly indicated that President Obama had nothing to do with the IRS's actions, yet he was still eviscerated by the GOP and news media. On this point, MSNBC commentator Martin Bashir shared an interesting perspective: "Despite the complete lack of any evidence linking the president to the targeting of Tea Party groups, Republicans are using it as their latest weapon in the war against the black man in the White House" (Huffington Post 2013).

Ironically, it was reported that during the time frame in question, the IRS approved more conservative groups for tax-exempt status than liberal groups by a two-to-one margin (Blumenthal 2013).

Umbrella-Gate

On May 16, 2013, while delivering an address on the White House lawn, President Obama requested that umbrellas be held to shield him and his dignitary guest from rain while they delivered their respective addresses. The umbrellas were held by two US Marines. President Obama was criticized by the press and the GOP for the use of the Marines in such a manner. However, Presidents H. W. Bush and G. W. Bush were each protected by an umbrella held by a uniformed US Army soldier as they delivered their respective addresses in the rain (Google). What was the difference between the Bushes' and Obama's umbrella protection, and where was the criticism for the Bush occurrence?

As an outcome of the AP and IRS incidents, some Republicans and pundits compared President Obama to President Nixon. In my opinion, there is no comparison. President Nixon disgraced the presidency by authorizing illegal monitoring of American citizens; he was also accused of authorizing or condoning illegal breaking and entering, along with other illegal actions. Despite these allegations, after Nixon resigned from office, President Ford pardoned him. And yet there was talk in some conservative circles about impeaching President Obama for events in which, unlike Nixon, he had no personal or criminal involvement.

In closing, were the reactions to the AP, Benghazi, IRS, and Umbrella-Gate incidents race-neutral political maneuvering, contrived racist manipulation, or a combination of both? History will form its own conclusions.

Three-Party Political System

"Less Democrat—Less Republican—More Constitution"
(The Tenth Amendment Center 2013)

Now may be the time for a third major political party. Independents comprise approximately one-third of the voting population and appear to be growing. According to numerous polls, Americans are becoming disenchanted and frustrated with the Democratic and Republican parties, and their continual unwillingness to compromise with each other on key issues. Both parties appear to have lost sight of a 1991 admonition delivered by then–Arkansas Governor Bill Clinton during a Democratic Leadership Council event, an admonition that holds true today for all political parties. Said Clinton, "We have got to have a message that touches everybody, that makes sense to everybody, that goes beyond the stale orthodoxies of left and right—one that resonates with the real concerns of ordinary Americans, with their hopes and their fears" (Democratic Leadership Council 1991).

In present-day elections under the two-party system, Independents are the weakest, with few elected. Independents have to campaign in either the Democratic or Republican primaries or independently run on their own, without major-party support, as Ross Perot (Reform Party) did during the 1992 presidential campaign. Independents may currently be weak in elections, but then again, who thought the fledgling US Olympic hockey team would defeat the undefeated USSR team in the 1980 Olympics or that the British would lose the Revolutionary War?

I have read several articles written by pundits opposed to a three-party system; however, an increasing number of Americans disagree. A 2010 Gallup article suggests a growing preference for a three-party political system:

> Given the lack of alternatives, it perhaps is no surprise that Americans' desires for a third party are as high as they've been in at least the last seven years. And while the formation of an official third party is not imminent, that desire may be manifested in voters' strong anti-incumbent sentiments this year. (J. M. Jones 2010)

After the Gallup article was written, the 2010 midterm elections occurred. Due to uncertainty about President Obama's economic policies and the staggering unemployment rate, Democratic incumbents experienced major setbacks resulting in a majority-Republican House of Representatives with Democrats barely holding the majority in the Senate, setting the stage for unprecedented political gridlock and divisiveness. Since there are currently only two mainstream political parties, bouncing back and forth between two opposing political ideologies and not having other viable options are wearing thin.

In 1958, then–US Senator John F. Kennedy stated, "Let us not despair but act. Let us not seek the Republican answer or the Democratic answer but the right answer. Let us not seek to fix the blame for the past—let us accept our own responsibility for the future" ("Ready Reference: John F. Kennedy Quotations"). Let's seek the right answer by adding Independents as a third major political party. Can it get any worse than it is now?

Voter Intimidation by Employers

I discussed voter suppression in the "Racism" section of chapter 1, "Classism and Racism," because from my perspective there was sufficient evidence to conclude that voter suppression attempts were racially motivated. Even though a racial component is present with some employers, I cannot make the same determination about voter intimidation by all employers. Therefore, I will discuss this as a race-neutral by-product of the Supreme Court's *Citizens United* ruling.

During the 2012 presidential campaign, several Republican corporate CEOs sent employees e-mails and other communications "urging" them to vote for Romney and donate money to his campaign. For example, the Koch brothers (owners of Koch Industries) sent such a communication to forty-five thousand employees—a communication made legal by the Supreme Court's *Citizens United* ruling (Elk 2012). This highlights a disturbing trend in corporate America, as described in excerpts from the online daily publication *BeyondChron*:

> The Koch's in-house campaigning for the GOP is part of a larger trend of corporations exercising new freedoms under *Citizens United*. The Supreme Court decision overturned previous FEC laws prohibiting employers from expressing electoral opinions directly to their employees . . .
>
> Ironically, while the Kochs have been taking advantage of *Citizens United* to expand political communications to

employees, they have also capitalized on weak labor laws to limit the political speech of those employees. (Elk 2012)

Because of the *Citizens United* ruling, the Koch brothers had a legal right to express their political beliefs to their employees; however, in communicating such beliefs, there was an implied threat associated with their "suggestions." There is an unwritten, yet powerful axiom in the military that also exists in many corporate environments—the suggestion of the commander is in fact an order. In the case of the Koch brothers, the implied message to their employees was to vote for President Obama at their own risk—a form of legal intimidation under color of the First Amendment, *Citizens United* ruling, and at-will employment relationship.

In at-will states, where an employer can discharge employees without showing cause, the consequences of not following the "suggestions" are very real. As a perfect example, Terry Lee, owner of Terry Lee Forensics in the at-will state of Utah, laid off two employees for voting for President Obama and supporting Obamacare. To explain his actions, Lee commented, "We had to let two employees go to cover new Obongocare [Obamacare] costs and increased taxes . . . Found two Obongo [Obama] supporters and gave them the news yesterday. They wanted the idiot in the Whitehouse [sic], they reap the benefits" (Gordon 2013). Firing employees for supporting "Obongo," "Obongocare," and the "idiot in the Whitehouse [sic]"—need more be said?

Did the *Citizens United* ruling open a Pandora's Box that legalized the intimidation of employee voters? Hopefully, the *Citizens United* ruling will eventually be reversed, thus allowing employees to vote without coercion as the Constitution intended.

Chapter 4

SOCIOECONOMIC

How do I feel about my country?

America is slowly recovering from the 2008 recession, but still suffering from a socioeconomic malaise. Consider the rising costs of education, health care, and insurance premiums, an endangered social entitlement system, a sluggish economy, the lack of an approved federal budget since 2009, the loss of America's Standard and Poor's AAA credit rating, and the draconian federal sequestration spending cuts that occurred due to congressional intransigence. America's workforce continually endures the transfer of manufacturing capability and jobs to other countries and an improving, but still high unemployment rate.

It is more difficult and dangerous for parents to raise their children than it was decades ago. The news media, instead of being uplifting and optimistic, paints a pessimistic picture of America. Americans are inundated with TV reality shows that profit from displaying the worst people can do or say to each other, and is it any wonder why children display a corresponding lack of respect and civility? Lastly, there are contentious debates regarding abortion, gun control, and the rights of gay Americans.

America is falling behind other industrialized nations in key measures of infrastructure, health, and education, and also has the largest debt in the world. This prompts a very disturbing question. Is America still the number one country in the world? Answering this question would require its own book, which is why I will confine my comments to a few socioeconomic issues that concern me—some mainstream and some not:

- Gun Control
- Line-Item Veto
- Parenting

- Pro-Choice v. Pro-Life
- Same-Sex Marriage
- Separation of Church and State
- Sin Taxes
- Social Entitlements
- The News Media

During the 2012 presidential campaign, the GOP asked if America was better off since President Obama took office. A more appropriate question would have been to ask where America was when Republican President G. W. Bush left office as compared to where America is now under President Obama's leadership. During his keynote speech at the 2012 Democratic National Convention, President Clinton answered this question:

> I like the argument for President Obama's reelection a lot better. He inherited a deeply damaged economy, put a floor under the crash, began the long hard road to recovery, and laid the foundation for a modern, more well-balanced economy that will produce millions of good new jobs, vibrant new businesses, and lots of new wealth for the innovators . . . Are we better off than we were when he took office, with an economy in free fall, losing 750,000 jobs a month? The answer is *yes*. (DNC2012 2012)

In spite of my concerns, I am comfortable with President Clinton's assessment. It appears America may be going in the right direction, with a slowly decreasing unemployment rate and the federal government reporting a rare surplus of $116.5 billion in June 2013, the largest in five years. This surplus keeps the nation on track for its lowest annual deficit in five years (Associated Press 2013). However, time will tell.

Gun Control

Gun-control opponents repeatedly state that guns do not kill people; people kill people. I totally agree; however, America has a serious problem regarding gun-related violence that must be addressed. The

Internet magazine *Slate* has been tracking gun-related deaths since the Sandy Hook school tragedy and paints an alarming picture of gun violence in America. Using the most recent Centers for Disease Control and Prevention estimates for yearly deaths by guns in America, it is likely that as of September 25, 2013, roughly 25,379 people have died from guns since the Sandy Hook shootings, as compared to approximately 8,694 deaths reported in the news (Kois and Kirk 2013). It would be safe to assume that the actual level of gun-related deaths in America is grossly understated. Let's examine some additional facts.

Bath School (45 killed), Virginia Tech (33 killed), Sandy Hook Elementary School (26 killed), University of Texas (16 killed), Columbine High School (15 killed), Red Lake Senior High School (8 killed), Amish School (6 killed), and Northern Illinois University (6 killed)—these are just a few of several school shootings that resulted in six or more deaths since 1927 ("List of school shootings in the United States"). These incidents do not take into account the hundreds of thousands of other gun-related homicides, suicides, and injuries that have occurred since the beginning of the twentieth century.

On a broader note, PBS political commentator Mark Shields claims more Americans have been killed by gunfire since 1968 than in all the major wars in America's history. PolitiFact.com, a Pulitzer Prize-winning website, validated his claim with the following findings. From the Revolutionary War to Afghanistan, 1,171,177 Americans have died in major wars as compared to 1,384,171 killed by gunfire in America since 1968. An additional 362 Americans have died from military interventions in Grenada, Haiti, Lebanon, Panama, and Somalia, but this number is not large enough to make a difference in the comparison (PolitiFact.com 2013).

As further background, the number of gun-related homicides is higher in America than almost all other developed countries. The only developed country with a higher rate is Mexico due to drug cartel wars. In 2009, there were three homicides committed with a firearm per 100,000 inhabitants in America. By comparison, the rate for the UK, where handguns are prohibited, was 0.07 per 100,000, and Germany's rate was 0.2 per 100,000. However, Switzerland has one of the highest gun ownership rates in the world, with 1.2 to 3 million guns in the private residences of approximately 8 million citizens, yet in 2006, Switzerland had a firearm homicide rate of 0.25 per 100,000

("Gun Violence in the United States"). It would be safe to conclude that given this homicide rate disparity between America and the rest of the developed world, something needs to be done to curb gun violence in America. Consequently, I support gun control as a viable solution, but others do not.

Central to the gun-control debate is the interpretation of the Second Amendment to the Constitution. The Second Amendment states: "A well regulated militia, being necessary to the security of a free State, the right of the people to keep and bear Arms, shall not be infringed." Gun-control opponents use a "protect against government tyranny" rationale as one of several arguments against gun control. Granted, the Revolutionary War was the result of colonialists raising arms against a tyrannical British monarchy, and despite various quotes from some of the Framers of the Constitution (such as Jefferson, who mentioned tyranny while discussing the right to keep and bear arms), the Second Amendment does not contain the word "tyranny" or imply that tyranny was the primary reason for writing the Second Amendment. Granted, one of several indisputable reasons for writing the Constitution was to protect Americans from the tyranny of government; however, there is no conclusive evidence that clearly establishes the Framers' overarching motive for specifically writing the Second Amendment. In addition to the need for state militias, there are other plausible motives:

- enabling participation in law enforcement activities
- enabling individual self-defense and defense of the home or family
- protecting against foreign invasions or attacks and domestic insurrection

When debating the Second Amendment, do not blindly rely on the Framer's principled intent, which could arguably be characterized as disingenuous and self-serving, regarding the right to keep and bear arms. Since the Framers were mostly rich white property owners, the Second Amendment could be construed as the Framers' attempt to provide constitutionally mandated protection for their property and slave-owning status, thus planting the seeds for perpetual class warfare and a future civil war. Additionally, examine the Framers' intent regarding self-evident truths, as outlined in the Declaration of Independence, i.e.

"that all men are created equal, that they are endowed by their creator with certain unalienable rights, that among these are life, liberty and the pursuit of happiness," while George Washington, almost half of the Framers including Jefferson and Madison, and a super-majority of southern property owners owned slaves. Also, in addition to slaves, women, non-property-owning white males, and indentured servants were not allowed to vote in many parts of colonial America. It is very plausible that the Framers were equally or more concerned about ensuring their own personal safety from domestic insurrection by disenfranchised constituencies than providing protection from the tyranny of government.

The similarities between the Framers and present-day white gun-control opponents are undeniable with regard to their stated needs to ensure a constitutional right to keep and bear arms for reasons of self-defense and protection against tyranny of government. However, for gun-control opponents, it could be argued that the current opposition to gun control is being fueled by the fears of a shrinking white constituency that may soon become a numerical minority in America. From another perspective, while watching televised coverage of gun shows, other events sponsored by gun-control opponents, and doomsday prepper reality shows, it is interesting that the presence of people of color, especially African Americans, is extremely rare—at least on camera.

With this background, let's focus on gun-related problems in present-day America. For me, the problems are not the firearm models (AK47, AR15, etc.), high-capacity magazines, or the amount of purchased ammunition. The problems are the glorification and promotion of gun violence through violent and profitable video games and similar media, a socioeconomic infrastructure that prompts violence in low-income inner-city locales, and the semiautomatic functionality that enables a high rate of fire. The First Amendment makes it extremely difficult to address media-generated violence, and America has yet to adequately address the economic plight of the poor and disenfranchised or firearm capabilities.

The Supreme Court's 2008 *DC v. Heller* ruling permits the banning of assault weapons meant for the military and restricting private firearm ownership to the types in use at the time the Second Amendment was ratified—a time that did not include semiautomatic or automatic firearms (Whelan 2008). The majority opinion states, in part:

> The Second Amendment right is not unlimited. We do not cast doubt on concealed-weapons prohibitions, laws barring possession of firearms by felons and the mentally ill, laws barring firearms in sensitive places like schools and government buildings, and laws imposing conditions on commercial sale of arms. Also, the sorts of weapons protected are the sorts of small arms that were lawfully possessed at home at the time of the Second Amendment's ratification, not those most useful in military service today, so 'M-16 rifles and the like' may be banned. (Whelan 2008)

In my opinion, the total elimination of military-grade assault weapons is not a solution. As a chemist can subtly change an illegal drug's molecular structure such that the drug is again technically legal; the same could happen with changing the characteristics of a firearm such that it is legally not considered an assault weapon. The Second Amendment does not address and, by omission, permits the regulation of firearm functional capabilities as long as such regulation does not infringe the constitutional right to keep and bear arms—a technicality, but a very important one. Given this constitutional loophole and as an alternative to the total elimination of assault weapons, *ban the semiautomatic functionality*, restricting this functionality to law enforcement, security and intelligence agencies, and the military. Convert currently owned semiautomatic assault weapons and extend this ban to the future manufacturing and sale of firearms. Rather than fighting a losing battle with the gun lobby to eliminate assault weapons, if constitutionally within his purview to do so, President Obama should ban the semiautomatic functionality via an executive order. In 1978, in response to the OPEC oil embargo and to reduce national gas consumption, President Nixon issued an executive order mandating a nationwide 55 mph maximum speed limit.

There is a very distinct advantage to removing the semiautomatic functionality. Via the manual operation of an assault rifle's cocking/charging handle or a shotgun's pump action, a shooter would have to manually extract a spent round and seat the next round, thus reducing the high rate of fire associated with semiautomatic assault weapons. Converted firearms would no longer be considered assault weapons—just exotic-looking rifles that look like, but do not have the capability of military-grade assault weapons. They would be neutered knockoffs. This would render the assault weapons argument moot. Also, consider banning semiautomatic pistols, thus making revolvers the only handguns that can be purchased for private ownership. With revolvers, the concerns about handgun high-capacity magazines would also become moot.

As a contingency, if banning semiautomatic firearms is not technically feasible, regulate them in the same manner as automatic weapons. The private ownership of automatic weapons is regulated by Title II of the 1968 Gun Control Act, requiring attorney general approval and federal registration *prior* to ownership, and a federal tax upon each transfer or making of an automatic weapon ("Title II Weapons").

As I and others I know who are skilled with firearms will attest, the semiautomatic functionality is not necessarily required by a proficient shooter for hunting, most in-home defense scenarios, or other close-quarter self-defense encounters (military and law enforcement combat scenarios are obvious exceptions). It is also my belief that most assault weapon buyers purchase such weapons for cosmetic or name appeal versus functional requirements, or as several potential gun buyers answered at a televised gun show when asked why they liked assault weapons: "They look cool." Doomsday preppers and private militias will probably disagree with my assessment, believing they need military-grade firearms in order to protect their homes and families from apocalyptic events or government tyranny. I will concede that if such events occur, their preparation will have been appropriate; however, since I do not expect such events in the foreseeable future, I will not consider the prepper and militia perspectives as I continue this discussion.

On an economic note, the complete elimination of assault weapons could have a negative impact on gun manufacturers and related small businesses, resulting in the loss of jobs and business closures. Retooling gun manufacturing operations to convert existing and produce new firearms without the semiautomatic functionality could save and create jobs, and protect gun-manufacturer profitability and related small businesses while enhancing public safety—a win-win proposition.

Removing or regulating the semiautomatic functionality is only one of several steps needed to curb gun violence. Mull over these additional recommendations for a comprehensive gun-control strategy:

- *Vigorously* enforce existing gun-control laws.
- Given the *DC v. Heller* ruling and since the Second Amendment does not prohibit the taxation of firearms, do not place limitations on the amount of firearms and ammunition that can be purchased by an individual—just tax excess ownership. For example, establish a penalty-free limit of one pistol, one shotgun, and one rifle per eligible adult, and levy a hefty one-time-only federal tax on every privately owned firearm that exceeds these limits. There are precedents for this approach—a person can purchase an unlimited amount of properties, but can only claim one property as a principal residence for tax purposes. Additional properties beyond the principle residence are taxed differently.
- Establish a one- or two-year amnesty and national buy-back program. During this amnesty period, excess firearms can be turned in, no questions asked, with fair compensation given to the owner, and retained firearms can be converted to remove the semiautomatic functionality.
- Fund the development of and mandate smart technology, such as tamper-proof pistol grip safety locks. For example, imprint a firearm with the registered owner's palm and fingerprints such that the firearm will only fire if held by the owner. There are precedents for this requirement; for example, the mandatory requirement that all cars have seat belts, air bags, and catalytic convertors, or the use of biometric data by various government agencies and businesses for identification and security purposes.
- Mandate the compulsory registration of all firearms along with a fired bullet's rifling impressions and striations when manufactured, all stored in a database similar to law enforcement's national DNA and fingerprint databases. When a weapon is purchased, the gun's registration would be linked to the owner. The precedent for this is the vehicle identification number registration of all vehicles when manufactured and subsequent linkage to the owner after purchase.
- Require mandatory background checks on all prospective firearms buyers during all firearm transactions. The 1968 Gun Control Act prohibits gun possession by persons meeting certain criteria, such as felons and the mentally ill. These provisions were supported by the NRA when the Gun Control Act was

enacted ("National Rifle Association"). Mandatory background checks would enhance official capabilities to prevent firearm purchases by prohibited individuals.

- As a prerequisite to owning a firearm, require gun safety classes that include a shooting proficiency test for all first-time firearm owners who do not have verifiable military, security, or law enforcement firearm experience. The precedents for this are the mandatory written and driving tests that must be passed by first-time drivers in order to get a license. Additionally, a licensed driver must pass a separate set of written and driving tests before being allowed to operate a motorcycle or commercial vehicles.

- Consider mandating low-velocity hollow-point ammunition for personal and in-home defense. High-velocity rounds, especially hot-loads such as the 357 Magnum and large caliber (40, 44, 45, and 50 caliber) rounds, have a tendency to pass through a human body, wall, or door, and can strike an innocent bystander. Low-velocity hollow-point ammunition expands on impact and will usually not pass through the human body or other solid objects unless fired at an extremely close range to the target. The precedents for this would be the ongoing research conducted by the Secret Service Presidential Protection Division into low-velocity ammunition that has the appropriate stopping power, but will not pass through a target's body and strike a bystander, or various military special operations units using low-velocity ammunition that will not penetrate walls and strike innocent noncombatants in another room. The military cannot use hollow-point ammunition due to restrictions imposed by the 1989 Hague Convention.

- Even though high-capacity magazine concerns would be rendered moot if the semiautomatic capability was removed, I would not oppose restrictions on magazine capacities.

- Since the Second Amendment does not address the manufacture and sale of firearms, implement the following:
  o Eliminate federal firearms licenses that allow private citizens or collectors to engage in the interstate and intrastate sale of weapons and ammunition.

o   Eliminate the private-sale loopholes that permit the purchase of firearms without a background check.
o   As some states regulate the sale of alcohol via state liquor stores, mandate similar government regulation of gun manufacturing, repair, and sales through the establishment of state or federal gun stores. Mandate federal prison sentences for the sale, repair, or manufacturing of weapons and ammunition outside of the regulated system.

As an opponent of gun-control efforts, the NRA can espouse the Second Amendment all it wants, but would not have a constitutional leg to stand on, since my proposals do not infringe on the right to keep and bear arms. The NRA needs to remember that when the Constitution was written, the Framers lived in a world where a colonialist, if armed, only carried *one* musket, maybe *one* pistol, and *one* knife that was sometimes supplemented with *one* hatchet or tomahawk. Also, many colonialists did not own or have an interest in firearms until they were required to have specified weapons and ammunition in accordance with the Second Militia Act of 1792. Again, the Framers had no concept of automatic or semiautomatic firearms; firearm functional capabilitieswere not being specifically addressed when the Constitution was ratified.

To be fair, some of the NRA's concerns are shared by a significant number of Americans, as explained in an article by Scott Coffina from the *National Review Online*:

> [The NRA] represents the serious concerns of millions of law-abiding Americans, from both parties, who value their Second Amendment right to gun ownership for self-defense, sport, and protection against disorder or government tyranny, as the Framers originally intended. The President once derisively talked about 'bitter' small-town residents 'cling[ing] to guns or religion.' Well, nothing would make people cling harder to their guns than an effort to ban them by executive fiat [order]. (Coffina 2013)

This is all well and good, but let's remember that gun-control legislation does not call for a *total* ban on private firearm ownership, nor is such a ban being considered by executive order. Without discussing linguistic arguments concerning the Framers' use of the words "bear arms," there is a universal understanding that the Second Amendment right to keep and bear arms is sacrosanct (Gun Control Act restrictions noted). Regarding "executive fiat," since the Sandy Hook shooting, President Obama has signed several innocuous executive orders that buttress existing gun-control laws and regulations and establish research and data-collection efforts to quantify the impacts of gun violence.

In accordance with the 1952 Supreme Court *Youngstown Sheet & Tube Co. v. Sawyer* ruling (Coffina 2013), President Obama cannot eliminate the entire class of assault weapons via executive order because such an action falls within the purview of Congress. Herein is the problem—congressional intransigence. The gun lobby has been very effective in influencing congressional lawmakers. An example of this influence was the April 17, 2013, Senate vote that failed to stop the filibuster of an amendment expanding background checks before purchasing a firearm, even though opinion polls indicated a majority of Americans were not opposed to such checks. Former Representative Gabrielle Giffords, who was shot in the head in 2011, scolded the senators who voted against the amendment:

> The US Senate decided to do the unthinkable about gun violence—nothing at all . . . Over two years ago, when I was shot point-blank in the head, the US Senate chose to do nothing. Four months ago, twenty first-graders lost their lives in a brutal attack on their school, and the US Senate chose to do nothing. It's clear to me that if members of the US Senate refuse to change the laws to reduce gun violence, then we need to change the members of the US Senate. (Wing 2013)

The senators who voted nay should consider the thousands of gun-related deaths that have occurred in America in just nine months since the Sandy Hook tragedy.

During anti–gun control events, conservative NRA spokesman and actor Charlton Heston would repeat renditions of an anti–gun control slogan while holding a vintage musket aloft: "You can have my gun when you pry it from my cold, dead hands." Heston died peacefully in bed, from pneumonia, without a gun in his hand; however, it is difficult to take solace in the fact that he died peacefully while other Americans are wounded or killed by gunfire on a daily basis.

In sharp contrast to conservative Heston, celebrity rapper and actor Snoop Lion (formerly known as Snoop Dog) embraced the violent "gangsta" genre throughout his career. In 2013, he experienced a cathartic transformation that resulted in the recording of "No Guns Allowed," a powerful video decrying gun violence. Whether or not Snoop Lion's transformation is sincere, the "No Guns Allowed" video is reflective of the transformation gun-control opponents need to undergo to stop the madness of unabated gun violence in America.

Guns do not kill people. People kill people, and semiautomatic firearms and the lack of a comprehensive gun-control strategy make it easier to do. My message to President Obama and Congress is to cease the rhetorical tit-for-tat and get gun control done. The "I care about yours and your children's safety" pontificating is getting old, and the NRA needs to realize that NRA could potentially be translated as **N**ot **R**ight for **A**merica.

Line-Item Veto

Currently, the federal budget must be approved or vetoed in its entirety because the president does not have line-item veto authority. The president should have line-item veto authority in accordance with the 2006 proposal by President G. W. Bush. In this proposal, for the president to withdraw specific provisions, a simple majority of Congress would be required to agree with deletions recommended by the president and filibustering would not be allowed. This proposal failed to get congressional support. As a result, the last time a federal budget was approved was in 2009, and it is now the second half of 2013.

Continual partisan infighting about earmarks, pork, income taxes, and federal spending has stalemated the budgetary process to the point of being an exercise in futility—all at the expense of middle-class and poor Americans. In order to fund the continued operation of the government, stop-gap measures are enacted to enable the government to pay the bills and borrow money. This is not the way to conduct business. The all-or-nothing approach to approving a budget results in nothing being accomplished. The inability to compromise and agree on a fiscal policy and budget has caused America to lose its Standard and Poor's AAA credit rating. If this trend continues, America may be downgraded again, all resulting in investors questioning or losing confidence in America's good faith and credit.

The line-item veto would allow portions of the federal budget to be enacted. For example, President Obama and the Republicans agreed on lowering the tax rate on corporations, yet disagreed on an income tax rate increase on the rich. A line-item veto would have allowed President Obama to sign a new corporate tax rate into law while continuing to debate the income tax rate. The line-item veto would also end the political extortion that occurs when an unpopular provision is included in high-profile legislation. As another example, the 2013 National Defense Authorization Act contained provisions that would limit Obama's and the military's ability to move and disposition incarcerated terrorists and alleged terrorists, thus negating President Obama's efforts to close the Guantanamo Bay Detention Center. If Obama vetoed the legislation because of these provisions without a line-item veto, he would in effect be vetoing the entire defense budget. A final example was the federal aid package for Hurricane Sandy victims. Unrelated provisions were added to the package that resulted in various lawmakers voting against it, delaying aid to New Jersey and other impacted areas. A line-item veto would have prevented this from happening. The complete package could have been presented to President Obama, and he would have the option to accept or reject the provisions. If he vetoed various provisions, Congress would have the opportunity to address the vetoed provisions without delaying the approved portion of the package that contained the aid.

Line-item veto authority makes sense, and the political rationale for not getting this done still escapes me.

Parenting

There is an African proverb that it takes a whole village to raise a child. As far as I am concerned, because of increased violence and government meddling into parental affairs, it now takes the whole village *plus a miracle* to raise a child in America. Please consider the following scenarios.

A teenage daughter breaks a major rule and the father grounds her. One day, the doorbell rings, and there is a Division of Youth and Family Services representative with two police officers. In reaction to the grounding, the daughter called 1-800-911-KIDS and falsely accused the father of abusing her. Realizing the gravity of the situation, the daughter recants and tells the truth. The authorities leave after lecturing the father and daughter and reminding them about the potential legal consequences of rendering a false report.

An adolescent son is disrespectful and spanked on the butt with a belt by his father—hurt, but not injured. Parents who choose to administer corporal punishment should *never* injure or endanger their child. He goes to school the next day and, while wearing gym shorts, the gym teacher notices a black and blue imprint on the back of his thigh. He is taken to the principal's office, and tells the truth about being spanked for being disrespectful, but the authorities are called anyway. The father is arrested and charged with child abuse. The ending to this story will depend upon the inclinations of the authorities and the laws of the jurisdiction where the parent was arrested.

Is there any wonder why parents are skittish about the methods used to discipline their children and that children sense the parents' reluctance and take advantage of it? Then the parents have to contend with supposed experts, pundits, and government officials telling them how to be good parents, and accusing the parents of being the fault for the lack of respect and questionable behaviors of their children. It seems parents are always guilty until proven innocent. This said, outside of the injury and endangerment exceptions, the government and judicial system need to *leave parenting to the parents.*

Another issue is the increasing number of latchkey children. A latchkey child comes home to an empty house because the parents are working. Latchkey children might have either a two-parent home or a one-parent home in which the single parent has to work one or two jobs to make ends meet. And, if a child gets in trouble while the parent is working, the parent is again lectured by judicial or government authorities on parental responsibilities for not being around enough to effectively monitor the child.

Single parents are caught in a classic catch-22 situation. If a single parent does not work in order to spend more time with the child, there will be no money for basic needs or living accommodations unless the parent applies for welfare, food stamps, or other government subsidies—which then results in the parent being labeled as a deadbeat drain on the system. If the parent works to support the family (which results in less time spent with the children) and a child gets in trouble, the parent is called irresponsible and chastised for not spending enough time with the child. Former First Lady Eleanor Roosevelt offered advice for such dilemmas, saying, "Do what you feel in your heart to be right—for you'll be criticized anyway. You'll be damned if you do, and damned if you don't" ("Eleanor Roosevelt Quotes").

On a different note, a teenage girl is pulled over by the police while driving a friend's car without a license. The offense requires a mandatory court appearance by the teenager and her parents. This is her first brush with the law, and the parents are loving and attentive. After administering punishment, the magistrate proceeds to admonish and lecture the parents on parental responsibilities. The magistrate is unmarried and without any children of his own. The child was wrong and deserving of judicial punishment, but again, there seems to be a presumption of guilt concerning parents. It is one thing for the magistrate to appropriately remind the parents about keeping a better eye on their child. It is a totally different matter when the magistrate, who does not know anything about the child's family structure or environment, embarrasses the parents in front of their child by giving a very condescending lecture on parenting, a subject on which he has absolutely no personal experience.

Then there are the low-income situations in which the father needs to be absent for the mother to get welfare money and Section 8 housing. Fathers struggling to provide for their families may leave the family for this reason, but regrettably many never return. With a splintered parental family structure where economic survival is the primary objective and the child also has to work or comes under the influence of other dubious moneymaking enterprises such as drug dealing, I would wager that there are direct correlations between the rate of juvenile delinquency, the state of the economy, and family income levels. But again, it is the fault of the parents—right?

There are a myriad of other social influences on a child, such as peer pressure, that compete with a parent's role in raising a child and share some of the responsibility for the state of youth today. What about the impacts of violent, misogynistic, or otherwise unrestrained mass media, such as radio, music videos, and reality TV, that push the envelope of civility and respect? For example, the Rah Digga song "Beat That Bitch with a Bat" immediately comes to mind. Did the Framers of the Constitution have this in mind?

The overall lack of civility and respect, children with guns, and the threat of being sued or arrested when interceding on the behalf of another child have all resulted in many parents avoiding interactions outside of their own immediate family circle. The erosion of our economy, the breakup of communities and family units, home foreclosures, gang and drug influences, dilapidated and underfunded educational infrastructures, and high unemployment all negatively impact a parent's ability to raise a child. Money (or lack thereof) is still the primary reason for divorce and single-parent homes. Is it any wonder why parents continue to operate at a deficit?

I agree that parents have the ultimate responsibility in raising a child, but our government needs to understand that it shares a lot of the blame for making a parent's job harder. Lawmakers can find billions of dollars for foreign aid and to fight wars, yet when it comes to funding the education of and infrastructure for our children, the issues are endlessly debated. Americans want to pass on the American Dream to our children, yet are we passing on an American nightmare?

Lastly, with the increased levels of disrespect and violence among today's youth, the distinction between a child and adult is becoming increasingly blurred. The innocence of America's youth is being lost, but again, the parents are at fault—right?

Instead of continually blaming the parents:

- Abolish 1-800-911-KIDS and similar numbers. Dialing 911 should be sufficient. The government needs to dial 1-FIX-ECO-NOMY to get parents back on their feet so they can properly provide for and raise their children.
- If lawmakers can add pork and earmarks to federal or state budget bills, they should be able to fund and staff DYFS and other child-related social, educational, protective, and community services as a priority, and not as an election-year afterthought.
- Remove the "absent father" requirement from welfare and related aid.
- Take a very hard look at TV reality shows that depict behaviors exhibiting a total lack of civility, respect, and deportment—a

negative influence on our children's behavior and social development. With the multiple means of access to the media via the Internet, television, and related mediums, parents cannot be expected to be the only moderators of what a child sees or hears.

Granted, there are parents who should not be raising children; however, an overwhelming majority of parents fulfill their parental responsibilities with love, attention, and care. What parents need is assistance, not constant blame and government regulation. When our government adequately funds and repairs critical institutions such as education, health care, and the overall economy, it will then have the moral authority to blame the parent. It should not take a miracle to raise a child in America. Provide parents with a stable and supporting infrastructure, and they (and the village) will do the rest.

Pro-Choice v. Pro-Life

Getting straight to the heart of the abortion debate, on May 29, 2013, El Salvador's Supreme Court ruled that Beatriz (a pseudonym), a twenty-two-year-old woman who was six months pregnant and seriously ill with lupus and kidney disease, could not have the abortion needed to save her life. Doctors determined in her first trimester that neither she nor her fetus was likely to survive the pregnancy. Additionally, her fetus had anencephaly—a birth defect that prevents the brain from fully forming. When Beatriz was fourteen weeks pregnant, her hospital asked permission from the authorities to perform an abortion because an abortion is a criminal offence in El Salvador (Bassett 2013). As a result of the court's ruling, both Beatriz and the unborn fetus would probably have died as a result of the pregnancy; however, she was finally granted permission to have a C-section, which was not considered an abortion since the pregnancy was so far along (Bassett 2013).

This story ended with Beatriz having the C-section, and the baby was born without a brain and died. Was this an acceptable outcome? If Beatriz was in America, under *Roe v. Wade*, she would have the right to choose, and an abortion would have been legally performed. What would have happened to Beatriz if *Roe v. Wade* had been overturned by the US Supreme Court?

After the 1973 *Roe v. Wade* ruling, I thought I was pro-life until I realized I had a problem reconciling the issue of choice. I am now pro-choice because I do not oppose abortions in the case of rape, incest, or if the mother's life is in danger and, by my logic, must therefore support a woman's universal right to choose even though I am opposed to abortions for all other reasons.

Prior to the *Roe v. Wade* ruling, states could mandate varying restrictions on when an abortion would be allowed. After *Roe v. Wade*, elective abortions became legal nationwide, with restrictions based on a "viability" determination:

> The *Roe* decision defined "viable" as being "potentially able to live outside the mother's womb, albeit with artificial aid," adding that viability "is usually placed at about seven months (28 weeks), but may occur earlier, even at 24 weeks. (*Roe v. Wade*)

This ruling resulted in the decades-long and volatile abortion debate. To better understand the impact of this debate, the following are statistics from a 2012 Gallup poll regarding Americans' abortion inclinations:

- Pro-Life: 50%
- Pro-Choice: 47%
- Should be legal under certain circumstances: 52%
- Should be legal under all circumstances: 25%
- Should be illegal under all circumstances: 22%

For pro-choice supporters, the argument is simple. By my understanding, a woman has a right to privacy that extends to her right to choose what happens to or in her body. For pro-life supporters, the argument is as follows:

> Pro-life advocates contend that elective abortion unjustly takes the life of a defenseless human being. This simplifies the abortion controversy by focusing public attention on just one question: Is the unborn a member of the human family? If so, killing him or her to benefit others is a serious moral wrong. (Klusendorf)

From a moral perspective, all human life is priceless, regardless of the nature or character of such life—whether metaphorically he or she is a saint or murderer. If the sanctity of all human life is the crux of the pro-life argument, pro-life-inclined states with the death penalty, such as Arkansas, Nebraska, Kansas, and Oklahoma, would be morally inconsistent and hypocritical in their application of the law. Executing a condemned inmate is in effect killing a defenseless human being, restraining the condemned such that they cannot defend themselves from being put to death—no different than the abortion of a fetus that is defenseless and trapped within the womb. In summary, death penalty states, the federal government, and the military have reserved the legal right to decide who is or is not executed—albeit after a court conviction for a capital crime. If state and federal entities can make such *choices* about human life, why can't a woman make similar choices regarding what happens to or in her body?

I would be remiss if I did not comment from a Christian perspective because religion is a major contributor to the emotional fervor on both sides of the argument. By my understanding, the Holy Bible does not expressly forbid or encourage abortion. However, in the Old Testament, there is no ambiguity associated with the "divinely authorized" killing of infants. Here are two of many examples:

> "Now go and strike Amalek and devote to destruction all that they have. Do not spare them, but kill both man and woman, child and infant, ox and sheep, camel and donkey." (1 Samuel 15:3, English Standard Version)

> Blessed shall he be who takes your little ones and dashes them against the rock! (Psalm 137:9, English Standard Version)

Assuming infants and "little ones" are considered defenseless, the distinction between the divinely ordered or blessed killing of infants and the voluntary abortion of the defenseless unborn would be an interesting religious debate. Lastly, Muslims regard abortion as wrong and *haram* (forbidden), but all schools of Islamic law accept that an abortion is permitted if the pregnancy threatens the mother's life (BBC 2009).

According to the 2012 Gallup poll, many Americans do not oppose abortions for rape, incest, or medical necessity, and herein lays the problem. If a pregnant rape victim can *choose* to have the baby or an abortion, *she is making a choice.* This is the very essence of the pro-choice position; a woman's right to choose. By my logic, if I support a rape victim's choice to have an abortion, I would be pro-choice even if I did not support abortions under any other circumstances. In other words, if I support one choice in one case, I am in effect supporting a woman's right to choose in *all* cases.

In my opinion, pro-life advocates who do not oppose various exceptions to the abortion rules are disingenuous with their opposition to *Roe v. Wade.* If the pro-life argument is based on the absolute protection of unborn life, from the time of conception, then the fate of unborn life cannot be subject to a choice. By my logic, to be an authentic pro-life advocate, one must oppose *all* abortions regardless of how the pregnancy occurred or the medical risk to the mother.

If the "supporting one choice supports all choices" logic was the basis for pro-choice/pro-life determinations, the aforementioned Gallup poll statistics would be adjusted as follows:

- Pro-Choice (abortions legal under all or certain circumstances): 77%
- Pro-Life (abortions illegal under all circumstances): 22%

These adjusted statistics would dramatically alter the abortion debate and clearly indicate the need to retain *Roe v. Wade.*

Same-Sex Marriage

In many southern states during the Jim Crow era, interracial marriage was banned by antimiscegenation laws. Keeping this in mind, what is the difference between discriminating based on skin color and discriminating based on sexual persuasion? Frankly, I cannot make the distinction.

Since marriage is not mentioned in the Constitution and if the separation of church and state principle is acknowledged, individual religious beliefs should not impact the constitutional requirement to ensure equal rights and protection for all Americans. I can understand why President Obama became the first president to publically support same-sex marriage. In addition to sharing the results of his own soul searching, President Obama was fulfilling his oath of office to defend the Constitution.

To set the stage for the continued legal debate on gay rights, in 2011, a federal appeals court ruled against Don't Ask, Don't Tell (DADT)—the military's ban on openly gay service members. This ruling resulted in the official termination of DADT and brings me to the Defense of Marriage Act (DOMA) that defined marriage as the legal union between a man and a woman. Section 3 of DOMA ordered the nonrecognition of same-sex marriage for federal entitlements, such as insurance benefits for government employees, Social Security survivor benefits, and the filing of joint tax returns. Several states piggybacked on DOMA by enacting similar laws or constitutional amendments.

The Obama administration concluded that Section 3 of DOMA was unconstitutional and, while continuing to enforce the law, no longer defended it in court ("Defense of Marriage Act"). In June 2013, the Supreme Court agreed with President Obama and, in a 5–4 ruling, ruled that DOMA was unconstitutional under the due process clause of the Fifth Amendment of the Constitution; however, the ruling did not address the constitutionality of same-sex marriages as legal unions. The Supreme Court also ruled on an appeal to repeal California's Proposition 8 law that banned same-sex marriage. In a 5–4 ruling, the court rejected the appeal and held that the same-sex marriage opponents who put Proposition 8 on California ballots in 2008 did not have the constitutional authority to defend the law in federal courts after California refused to appeal its previous loss at trial. This ruling opened the door for same-sex marriages in California, but did not address other states that ban same-sex marriages. The court left same-sex marriage bans in other states untouched (Huffington Post 2013).

Although I agree with the Supreme Court's DOMA ruling, I still have a problem with the use of the word "marriage." As a compromise, I have no issue with same-sex legal unions being called civil unions. Some may say "marriage" and "civil union" are just a play on words, but for me there is a clear distinction between the two. Even though marriage is a secular institution, the word "marriage" is an embedded part of my religious beliefs and the source of my ambivalence. Civil unions are often viewed by same-sex marriage supporters as "separate but equal," and opponents object because civil unions are nothing more than same-sex marriage by another name ("Defense of Marriage Act"). Both arguments are equally effective; however, I must remember my dislike for the ethnic descriptor "African American." Despite my discomfort, I still use it in public discourse and throughout *We the Who?* because it is the preferred phraseology in our social vocabulary. Should I treat the word "marriage" any differently?

To address the belief of some same-sex marriage opponents that homosexuality is a sin, remember the statement by Jesus in John 8:7 (King James Version), when he protects a woman from being stoned to death for committing adultery: "He that is without sin among you, let him first cast a stone at her." In other words, it is not for us to judge anyone—judgment is God's domain. This is clearly emphasized in Romans 12:19 (King James Version): "Vengeance is mine; I will repay, saith the Lord."

During the Civil War, President Lincoln commented on slavery and the North and South, invoking the name of God for victory:

> Both [North and South] read the same Bible and pray to the same God, and each invokes His aid against the other. It may seem strange that any men should dare to ask a just God's assistance in wringing their bread from the sweat of other men's faces, but let us judge not, that we be not judged . . . The Almighty has His own purposes. (Bartleby.com 1989)

Lincoln's comments could be reapplied to the "civil war" between advocates and opponents of same-sex marriage. Despite varying opinions by religious scholars, clergy, and pundits, who really knows God's purposes regarding same-sex marriage? The secular Constitution should be America's guide—a guide that, in my opinion, mandates equal rights for all, including the lesbian, gay, bisexual, and transgender community. As I juxtapose my religious beliefs with the Constitution and President Obama's comments, I cannot in good conscience object to the secular acceptance of same-sex marriage because, while it may not universally be considered morally or religiously acceptable, it is constitutionally obligatory.

This said, I am still ambivalent about same-sex marriage due to my religious beliefs; however, as stated earlier, my religious beliefs should not play a role in constitutional decisions regarding the equal rights of and protection for all Americans—an excellent transition to the next topic regarding the separation of church and state.

Separation of Church and State

In my opinion, it is not right to impose my religious beliefs on others, nor do I expect government to impose upon my religious beliefs. Consequently, I support a strict adherence to the separation of church and state, and will discuss the religious components of this discussion from a Christian perspective.

In Christian theology, Jesus spoke these words when asked if taxes should be paid to the Roman Empire and, by my interpretation, is a clear statement suggesting the separation of church and state: "Render therefore unto Caesar the things which are Caesar's; and unto God the things that are God's" (Matthew 22:21, King James Version).

Another biblical event can be interpreted as suggesting the separation of church and state. When Jesus violently cleared the holy temple of money changers and merchants, he stated that the temple was a holy place of worship and not a secular place of business, again suggesting the need to separate religious and secular activities.

Jump forward to colonial America. Even though not expressly included in the First Amendment, the Framers of the Constitution clearly feared the combination of state and religious power and prescribed a strict separation of the two. Because of this separation, America is a religiously diverse nation where religion and secular government coexist without major conflict. In 2007, the religious breakdown in America was three-quarters Christian, with the remainder practicing a non-Christian religion or having no religion or religious affiliation (The Pew Forum on Religion and Public Life 2007). Even though these statistics were from the year 2007, it is safe to assume they approximate America's religious composition in 2013.

Religion is an important part of American culture, but our government is not supposed to officially promote, endorse, or fund religious institutions or beliefs. By maintaining a strict separation of church and state, the freedoms of religious expression and practice are protected. However, the separation of church and state is still a hotly debated issue. Some believe government should endorse the religious values of various members of the religious community, such as the Christian majority, to the exclusion of all others; however, America is a democracy, not a theocracy. On this point, violations of the separation of church and state principle continually take place at many levels of government. Herein lies the problem. On too many occasions, America does not practice what it constitutionally preaches regarding the separation of church and state. For example:

- An Alabama judge opened court sessions with a Christian prayer and had to be compelled to remove a plaque of the Ten Commandments from his courtroom wall.
- Municipalities erected nativity scenes, crosses, menorahs, and other religious symbols to the exclusion of other faiths.
- On the National Day of Prayer, local authorities acting in their official capacities led citizens in prayer (ADL: Anti-Defamation League).
- The Pledge of Allegiance contains a reference to God.
- "In God We Trust" is inscribed on coin currency.
- During election years and to obtain votes, politicians pander to the beliefs of powerful religious segments, such as Evangelicals or the Christian majority as a whole.

In a democracy, the majority usually rules, but this does not apply to the application of the First Amendment protection concerning religion, which states that "Congress shall make no law respecting an establishment of religion, or prohibiting the free exercise thereof (The Charters of Freedom).

This protection equally applies to the minority of non-Christian religions and citizens without a religion or religious affiliation. Additionally, the Constitution makes no reference to active government involvement in religion. With one exception, religious phraseology does not appear in the Constitution. The exception is in the signatory section, where the date is written as "Seventeenth Day of September in the Year of *our Lord* one thousand seven hundred and Eighty seven" (The Charters of Freedom, italics mine).

With the noted exception, the intentional lack of religious phraseology reflects the Framers' intent that government should not be involved in religious matters to the extent that Article VI of the

Constitution also forbids religious tests as a qualification to hold federal office in America. If America is truly a nation of law and respects the rights of all religions and secular-oriented citizens, various changes would be necessary to practice what is constitutionally preached.

- Prohibit the open expression of religious inclinations, such as praying on government and publically funded properties and during related events. While on these properties or attending events, the individual right to privately or silently practice one's faith would remain intact.
- Remove all religious artifacts from government and publically funded properties and events.
- Even though the generic use of the word "God" is permissible under certain circumstances, remove all references to God from our currency and replace with the original motto of *E Pluribus Unum*. Similarly, remove the reference to God from the Pledge of Allegiance.
- Mandate affirming (making a secular promise) rather than swearing to God in all federal and state judicial and administrative actions requiring such an oath, to include the inaugurations of elected or appointed government officials.
- The president should stop the use of the Holy Bible, held by the chief justice of the Supreme Court (who is tasked with making objective judicial decisions regarding separation of church and state cases), while taking the oath of office. In my opinion, this is a conflict of interest that should require the chief justice and any other judges in similar circumstances to recuse themselves from all separation of church and state litigation.
- Replace the Holy Bible with a copy of the Constitution for the affirming of all elected officials. Oaths of office should require upholding the law and defending the Constitution, not defending the Bible or other religious texts such as the Islamic Quran or Jewish Torah.
- Remove religious terms from judicial language. For example, remove "Prayer for Relief" as the judicial phraseology for outlining requested damages or injunctive relief in a civil complaint because most, if not all, English-language definitions of prayer contain references to God or other religious deities.

Use secular phrases such as "Hope for Relief" or "Relief Requested."

As a Christian, this approach would still give me plenty of room to practice my religion as I deem appropriate. As distasteful as this may be to various religious factions, my suggestions are aligned with the Christian mandate to "render therefore unto Caesar the things which are Caesar's," and in compliance with the Constitution's intent to separate affairs of state from religion.

Two of the reasons the Mayflower Pilgrims immigrated to America were to escape state- and church-sponsored religious persecution in England, and to worship as they saw fit. The separation of church and state components of the Constitution were included in remembrance of this persecution because America cannot have it both ways by insisting on equal rights for all and then demanding religion-based exceptions to the rules. Nor can Americans advocate for the free and unabridged exercising of religion and then question someone's faith, as occurred when President Kennedy was questioned about being a Catholic or when President Obama felt obliged to proclaim he was a Christian and not a Muslim.

It is interesting how the wheel of history turns. Governments intruded on religious freedoms when the Roman Empire and Nazi Germany persecuted Christians and Jews, respectively. Conversely, religion intruded on these same freedoms when, during the Spanish Inquisition and with the approval of the Spanish monarchy, Catholic clergy punished or executed alleged heretics, unbelievers, and blasphemers. Could the same happen in present-day America? Americans should never forget the retribution directed at Muslims after 9/11, the Salem witch trials when alleged witches were executed in the name of God, or that slavery flourished in a supposedly free American society under color of the Constitution and also in the name of God.

Americans must also remember that all who do not learn from history's mistakes are doomed to repeat them.

Sin Taxes

Sin taxes are discriminatory, arbitrary, and capriciously applied taxes focused on products and services, such as tobacco, gambling, sodas, and alcohol that are discouraged for health, moral, and other reasons. I find it interesting that lawmakers chose the word "sin" to describe a secular tax. The religious connotation is obvious. In this regard, let's examine alcohol and tobacco from a Christian perspective with the understanding that other religions have differing opinions. Tobacco and alcohol usage may be frowned upon in some Christian denominations, but neither is a sin or considered immoral in most denominations. Wine is frequently used in the holy sacrament of Communion, and many priests smoke. Using a word with religious connotations to describe a secular law could be interpreted as a violation of the separation of church and state principle. A more appropriate and secular descriptor would be "vice tax."

To highlight the arbitrary and capricious application of sin taxes, why not apply a sin tax to the sale of pornography (not to say that some states have not tried to do just that)? Currently, pornography sales are regulated and taxed at the standard sales tax rates. If pornography is not considered socially reprehensible, politically incorrect, or morally deficient enough to warrant a sin tax, I do not know what is. Additionally, as a social drinker and former smoker, I think it is morally and ethically reprehensible for government to financially benefit from my legal addictions by taxing them. This is quintessential discrimination and should be considered unconstitutional.

The Independent Institute offered an interesting perspective regarding the implications of sin taxes:

> So-called 'sin taxes'—the taxing of certain products, like alcohol and tobacco that are deemed to be 'politically incorrect'—have long been a favorite way for politicians to fund programs benefiting special interest groups. But this concept has been applied to such 'sinful' products as soft drinks, margarine, telephone calls, airline tickets, and even fishing gear . . . In addition, the costs of selective taxation fall disproportionately on lower income groups while politically powerful special interest groups benefit. (The Independent Institute)

The application of a sin tax to promote the general welfare is an admirable reason for such a tax, if this is the true reason. In my opinion, the true intent of sin taxes is driven by greed. For example, if the concern is truly about our health, why not classify tobacco as a controlled substance? Doing so would restrict private ownership of tobacco products and remove a significant cause of escalating health care costs; however, it would also deprive federal and state governments of billions of dollars in tobacco tax revenue. Is government more concerned about Americans' health and moral inclinations, or making money? Another example is placing a sin tax on gambling in casinos while profiting from legal gambling via lotteries, such as Powerball and Mega Millions, and then increasing the incentive to play the lottery by not requiring state income taxes on winnings. *Is gambling appropriate only when the money suits our government?* Finally, a Cook County, Illinois, lawmaker wanted to enact a "violence tax" on the sale of firearms and bullets to help stem gun violence. On the surface, this suggestion sounds admirable, but is discriminatory and misplaced. This approach discriminates against law-abiding gun owners, takes attention away from law enforcement's need to up their game to quell the violence, and deflects government's responsibility to ensure that appropriate law enforcement and supporting socioeconomic infrastructures are in place and appropriately funded.

Discriminating against specific products and personal behaviors via the sin tax represents an ominous trend that can easily be extended into other areas of life. What is to prevent a sin tax on toilet paper, sun tanning, fast foods, or sugar? At the extreme, a few states were considering using vehicle-installed GPS monitors to tax driven miles. America's interstate highway infrastructure is funded by federal subsidies to the states, funding that comes from federal tax revenue. In other words, Americans pay to build the highways and would also have to pay to drive on them. Former Beatle George Harrison had similar concerns when he wrote the 1996 song "Taxman" while protesting British taxation policies. "Taxman" included lyrics that summarize my feelings about sin taxes:

> If you drive a car, I'll tax the street.
> If you try to sit, I'll tax your seat.
> If you get too cold, I'll tax the heat.
> If you take a walk, I'll tax your feet.
> (Harrison 1966)

In other words, any tax that exclusively targets a specific group or class of people is discriminatory, unconstitutional, and should be disallowed.

(In the previous gun-control discussion, I recommended a tax on privately owned firearms that may appear to contradict my call for the elimination of sin taxes. Sin taxes are levied on all purchases of a specific product or service. My gun-control proposal called for a tax only after a predetermined threshold of firearm ownership is exceeded—a small but important distinction.)

Social Entitlements

Former Vice President Hubert Humphrey once said that "the moral test of government is how that government treats those who are in the dawn of life, the children; those who are in the twilight of life, the elderly; those who are in the shadows of life, the sick, the needy, and the handicapped" ("Hubert Humphrey").

Our government will fail this test if it does not protect social entitlements such as Social Security and Medicare. If nothing is done, these entitlements could soon become insolvent. Permitting the insolvency of social entitlements would be an unforgivable and unconscionable breach of faith by the government. I now receive Social Security benefits, and the thought of losing them or having benefits drastically reduced infuriates me.

One of the reasons for the current condition of Social Security is a high unemployment rate, resulting in fewer workers paying FICA taxes. Another reason is the increase in life expectancy. In 1939, the average life expectancy was sixty-three, and in 2010, it was seventy-nine (Infoplease). This increase in life expectancy resulted in Social Security benefits being paid over a longer-than-anticipated period of time for each eligible person. Both reasons make sense, but did Congress contribute to Social Security's dire situation through the siphoning of funds?

The Social Security Trust Fund was created in 1939 for the purpose of investing the frequent surpluses created by the program's taxes into government securities. However, Congress raided this fund regularly due to a loophole. In 1983, this loophole was plugged as part of a Social Security reform package. Many critics claim that despite the 1983 reforms, Congress found ways to continue raiding the fund to pay for other programs. Note this dire prediction:

> The Treasury Department has for decades borrowed money from the Social Security trust fund to finance government operations . . . And at some point, perhaps as early as 2017, according to the CBO, the Treasury would have to start repaying the billions it has borrowed from the trust fund over the past 25 years, driving the nation further into debt or forcing Congress to raise taxes. (Steiner 2011)

Additionally, if the government takes the money as a loan, increases spending, and then increases taxes to pay back the loan with interest, the trust fund becomes an accounting gimmick and taxpayers are paying twice, with FICA taxes to provide funding and higher income taxes to pay back the spent money (Thomas).

As basic as my understanding of Social Security is, I have some simple ideas:

- Close loopholes that allow congressional use of the Social Security Trust Fund for funding other than its intended use, determine the amount of money syphoned by Congress, and mandate repayment back into the trust fund.
- Increase FICA taxes to compensate for the additional years Americans would receive Social Security and Medicare benefits due to a longer life expectancy.
- Mandate that all income taxes on unemployment benefits go directly into the Social Security Trust Fund.
- Increase the Federal Unemployment Tax Act contributions by corporate America. If corporations can fund exorbitant golden parachute severance packages for executives, they can help subsidize Social Security for their employees.

Despite my concerns, an overhaul of America's social entitlement system may be inevitable. It has been suggested that if modifications are made to Social Security, benefits for citizens who are fifty-five years of age and older at the time of the adjustment would not be affected. Consider increasing this cut-off age to sixty.

If social entitlements are drastically reduced or bankrupted, this would be an impeachable breach of promise committed by government officials who should have a fiduciary responsibility to manage the Social Security Trust Fund. Even with the promise that changes to Social Security benefits would not affect anyone fifty-five years old or older, the government signed an entitlement promissory note to we the people, and I expect the promissory note to be honored.

The News Media

> "Most people treat the news media like the exercise bike they have in their basement. They're glad it's there, but they never use it" (Curtis).

Until the 1990s, the news media enjoyed plenty of idiosyncratic credits with many Americans. If the news media reported it, it was assumed the information was credible and balanced—but not anymore. A 2012 Gallup poll indicates that Americans are rapidly losing confidence in television news. Twenty-one percent of adults said they had a "great deal" or "quite a lot" of confidence in television news, down 25 percent from 1993 (Huffington Post 2012). As articulated by award-winning journalist Juan González, this lack of confidence is clearly evident among Americans of color:

> The American people love to hate the media, in terms of their constant frustration with how newspapers and television and radio don't provide accurate coverage. But it's especially true among people of color. African Americans and Latinos and Native Americans and Asians have always felt denigrated and somehow misrepresented, deeply, by the American media system. (*Democracy Now!* 2011)

Even though the news media serves a valuable and informative purpose, it is changing into a politically partisan entity and a pessimistic conveyor of gloom, doom, and spin. Kashmira Lad wrote an article for *Buzzle.com* about the pros and cons of mass media (Lad). I modified an extract of the article to present my version of the pros and cons of the news media:

Pros:

- News media has a global audience, or it can reach a specified target group, via easily accessible television or the Internet.
- The news media is, for the most part, the only source of news outside of a person's locale.
- Certain types of news media have a loyal fan base and audience. For example, I exclusively watch CNN for national and international news, ABC for regional and local news, and ESPN for sports.
- News media can be used for educational purposes.

Cons:

- At times, the information reported may not be authentic from every angle. Hence, there may be misinterpretations or misrepresentations of the news. In this regard, the Trayvon Martin news coverage was a travesty due to premature rushes to judgment and inaccurate conclusions based on incomplete information and misguided speculation.
- News can be manipulated to influence the public. For example, a particular political party, interest group, or corporation may compel a major news organization to manipulate the news to their favor. Former CBS News anchor Dan Rather's comments about corporate media were very clear on this point. He said that "no more than six" companies control 80 percent of news distribution, and added:

> These large corporations, they have things they need from the power structure in Washington, whether it's Republican or Democrat, and of course the people in Washington have things they want the news to be reported. To put it bluntly, very big business is in bed with very big government in Washington and has more to do with what the average person sees, hears, and reads than most people know. (Huffington Post 2012)

- News media can be biased to reflect personal and political preferences at the expense of objective, fair, and balanced presentation of the news. For example, Rupert Murdoch, the CEO of News Corporation (the parent of Fox News) and a Libertarian, exerts a strong conservative influence over Fox News ("Media Bias in the United States").
- The news media no longer shares all the facts so the public can independently form their own opinions and conclusions. The news is presented in a manner that basically tells Americans what our opinions should be.
- Unnecessary sensationalism of a news item may project inaccurate and misleading messages that prompt wrong conclusions by the public or inflate the importance of a news item.

Under a combination of commercial profit and loss and political pressures, there is a trend within the news media that clearly indicates the traditional commitment to objectivity is giving way to the tendency to concentrate news coverage on biased interpretations of the facts—spin. This can be dangerous because spin can inundate the public with unreliable and agenda-promoting news coverage such that it becomes increasingly difficult to read between the lines, to separate facts and truth from the spin.

Certain news sources could be characterized as quasi-political action committees. When elements of the news media provide their own political opinions or spin, they are acting as political activists and not as journalists, and they should lose the protection of shield laws in the same manner that religious organizations would lose their tax-exempt status if they inappropriately participated in the political process. Additionally, the lack of objective and spin-free news can alienate the public and distort views on America, all mirroring the divisiveness that currently exists in our government. On the NBC's news and interview television program *Meet the Press,* Tom Brokaw made an interesting observation: "As I've gone around the country, a lot of people say to me, 'What's happened with the press? What's happened with political coverage in America? We don't feel connected to it'" (Huffington Post 2012). Brokaw also expressed concerns that the public is "tuning-out" Washington; however, spin is not the only concern.

News coverage seems to be about rape, pillage, plunder, murder, pedophilia, sexual abuse, corporate greed, malfeasance, domestic and global unrest, and other forms of gloom and doom—all the evil people do to each other. Of note is the news media's coverage of tragedies. After the Sandy Hook shooting, news outlets spent four-plus days with 24/7 television coverage, morbidly focusing on the pain and sorrow of the victims' next-of-kin and survivors. The on-scene reporters seemed to go out of their way to elicit and televise emotional and tearful reactions by asking insensitive or inane questions such as when a traumatized young girl was asked by a reporter, "Was everybody crying, scared, wanting their parents to come get them?" (Advertisement Journal 2012).

What did the reporter *think* they were feeling, that the children were laughing and in good cheer while being shot at? On many occasions, I have heard reporters ask the relatives of dead or injured victims how they felt about their loved ones being victimized. Questions like this indicate how insensitive the news media can be when reporters bottom-feed on misery, fear, and sorrow.

The protracted news coverage of Sandy Hook was frustrating and depressing. By comparison, in 2011, a military CH-47 Chinook helicopter was shot down in Afghanistan, killing *thirty* US soldiers. The news media gave the incident brief and respectful mention, and then quickly moved on—not the case with Sandy Hook. Granted, there is an emotional difference between innocent children being killed and soldiers dying in combat, but hopefully I made my point. Finally, some reporters would not speak the Sandy Hook shooter's name because they did not want to give him primetime attention. However, by continually focusing on the pain, suffering, and emotional damage of the tragedy, the reporters did exactly what they did not want to do. They gave the shooter the very attention he would have craved, had he lived.

The news media also focuses on the sorrow, fear, and human tragedy associated with acts of terror. Since one goal of terrorism is to inject fear into the targeted population, I could make a case that the news media subsidizes terrorism through journalism. What happened to American backbone, and not showing fear or shaky resolve in the face of adversity? After 9/11, conspicuous displays of national unity only lasted a few months before the general public and news media reverted back to business as usual—gloom and doom, the food that feeds terrorism's appetite.

Let's look at violence in general. In my opinion, Americans are in a state of depression or suffering from socioeconomic post-traumatic stress disorder. This prompts questions about the effects of constant exposure to depressing and violent news coverage without an equalizing counterbalance of uplifting and optimistic stories. CNN broadcasts the uplifting television awards program *CNN Heroes* once a year, but it is mostly gloom and doom for the rest of the year.

I cannot totally blame the news media. Violence sells, and the public is buying it. Nonviolent *Pac-Man* has long since given way to *World of Warcraft* and other violent and highly profitable video games. In the competition for ratings and advertising dollars, the news media seems to be following suit with doom-and-gloom news coverage because, again, it sells. To summarize, I observed a highly unusual event in the presentation of the news. On October 24, 2012, the "breaking news" tag appeared during a segment of CNN's morning television program *Newsroom*. Normally, this tag means a gloom-and-doom-related event has occurred; however, on this occasion, CNN news anchor Carol Costello smiled and made the memorable statement, "Hold on. This is *good* breaking news!" (CNN 2012). For Costello to have such an on-air reaction reinforces the validity of my comments regarding the expectation of gloom and doom from the news media.

On a different and unsettling note, the news media may be giving aid and comfort to America's enemies and putting our soldiers, intelligence agents, and others in danger by communicating classified or sensitive intelligence. The following are several examples:

- An Associated Press news article and other news sources revealed personal details that were leaked about a CIA double agent who prevented the underwear bombing of a passenger jet by al-Qaeda—probably signing his death warrant if al-Qaeda identifies him.
- The news media obtained leaked information and revealed the identity of the Pakistani doctor who played a crucial role in locating Osama bin Laden.
- The *New York Times* obtained leaked information and divulged information about a classified US cyber attack on Iran.
- When US Army Private First Class Bradley Manning leaked classified military and diplomatic materials to WikiLeaks (an

online organization whose sole purpose is to publish such information), the news media broadcasted what WikiLeaks made public. In my opinion, even though WikiLeaks shared information on the Internet, the news media should have shown more discretion and judgment by not rebroadcasting the material. In doing so, the news media broadened WikiLeaks' audience, further exposed America to attacks on its good name and reputation, and possibly endangered lives.

- In June 2013, Edward Snowden, a former National Security Agency employee, leaked classified material on domestic and global NSA surveillance programs to *The Guardian* and *Washington Post*. This leaked information was then communicated to the general public by these newspapers.

In light of these examples, consider this extract from a Congressional Research Service report to Congress:

> Press reports describing classified US operations abroad have led to calls from Congress for an investigation into the source of the leaks, and Attorney General Holder appointed two special prosecutors to look into the matter. The online publication of classified defense documents and diplomatic cables by the organization WikiLeaks and subsequent reporting by The *New York Times* and other news media had already focused attention on whether such publication violates US criminal law. (Congressional Research Service 2013)

The threat to military and intelligence personnel and diplomatic efforts should outweigh the public's right to know. The United States Code and the United States Code of Military Justice (for military personnel only) identify various crimes and punishments associated with the illegal disclosure of classified material and espionage; however, in my opinion, the unauthorized communication of classified material should be considered an act of treason. Accordingly, the offending individuals or news entities should be criminally prosecuted and compelled to reveal their sources as an exception to existing shield laws and related First Amendment protections.

At the grassroots level, the threat to innocent civilians should also outweigh the public's right to know. As an example, after the 2013 Boston Marathon bombing, to counter the inaccurate pictures of alleged bombing suspects communicated by the news media, the FBI released accurate pictures and warned the public to ignore all other photographs aired by news media such as the *New York Post* cover-page picture of two men that implied that the men may be the bombers—an inference that proved to be false. This prompts questions about irresponsible, shoddy, and shoot-from-the-hip journalism. This also raises a legal question. Hypothetically, if the men were injured or murdered via vigilante justice based on the published pictures, would the *New York Post* be criminally complicit in the men's injuries or deaths, and would depraved indifference apply?

As a final perspective regarding the news media not at its best, during the 2012 presidential campaign and without naming his source, Senate Majority Leader Harry Reid accused presidential candidate Mitt Romney of not paying income taxes for ten years. Anderson Cooper, anchor of the CNN television news show *Anderson Cooper 360°,* asked why Senator Reid would make such an accusation without presenting corroborating evidence or naming his source. Fair enough, yet the very next CNN story was an update on the violence in Syria. Cooper showed videos of the violence while proffering disclaimers that the authenticity of the videos could not be independently verified. It was interesting that Cooper challenged the authenticity of Senator Reid's unsubstantiated accusation while broadcasting unverified videos. Do as I say, not as I do?

With the exception of the racial bias that permeated the news media during the Jim Crow era, will the news media ever return to the days of Walter Cronkite (former CBS television news anchor) who, for many years, was considered the most trusted man in America, a period when the news was reported in a fair, balanced, and objective manner? Cronkite ended his CBS Evening News newscast with the phrase, "And that's the way it is," followed by the date. He omitted this signature phrase when he ended newscasts with his personal opinion, such as his iconic Vietnam War editorial after the Tet Offensive, because he did not want to confuse the objective and factual presentation of the news with subjective commentary or personal spin ("Walter Cronkite"). Oh, the good old days.

Chapter 5

US MILITARY

Soldiers train for war, but pray for peace.

Soldiers train for war, but pray for peace, or as originally attributed to ancient Roman writer Publius Flavius Vegetius Renatus, *si vis pacem, para bellum*—if you wish for peace, prepare for war ("Si vis pacem, para bellum"). In a parallel light, General Douglas MacArthur said, "The soldier, above all others, prays for peace, for it is the soldier who must suffer and bear the deepest wounds and scars of war" ("Douglas MacArthur Quotes").

Sometimes there will be war, with soldiers coming home less than whole or not at all. One would hope that if soldiers are put in harm's way, it would be for righteous reasons. To date, America has ended one conflict in Iraq and is still engaged in combat operations in Afghanistan. In my opinion, the reasons for invading Afghanistan (Operation Enduring Freedom) were righteous, but America's second foray into Iraq (Operation Iraqi Freedom) was not.

There have been questions about America's application of military force in general; however, if America deploys military force, the availability of advanced technology gives the military an overwhelming advantage, and is needed for this reason:

> Given the low-intensity urban, internecine conflicts likely to erupt for the foreseeable future, and the American public's expectation of low casualties, the best hope for the US to achieve its defense goals is to seize and maintain the same technological superiority with ground troops that served it so well in aircraft, tanks, and ships during the Cold War. (Knowles 2002)

Advanced technologies also require new rules for the conduct of war. One such rule is of concern—when to attack with armed drones if civilian noncombatants are at risk.

And finally, the conduct of war not only requires cutting-edge military technologies, strategies, and tactics, but also highly trained, disciplined, and motivated service members with high morale and an abiding sense of camaraderie to successfully prosecute all assigned missions. Contrary to these requirements and the maintenance of good military order and discipline, the leaking of classified material and sexual abuse have become troubling problems in the US military.

Given this introduction, consider my thoughts on the application of military force, drone attacks, military conflicts, and order and discipline.

Application of Military Force

Setting a good example is a far better way to spread ideals than through force of arms.—Ron Paul ("Ron Paul Quotes")

Since the deployment of nuclear bombs against Hiroshima and Nagasaki during WWII, nuclear weapons have reshaped the policies and protocols associated with the application of military force, most notably with the advent of the Mutually Assured Destruction (MAD) doctrine. In short, MAD serves as a deterrent and assumes that if one country attacks another with nuclear weapons, the attacked country will massively retaliate with nuclear weapons, resulting in the complete and mutually assured destruction of both countries. In short, nuclear weapons were and still are the equalizers in the conduct of international affairs and use of military force between nuclear superpowers and ideological rivals.

During the Cold War, America never attacked the nuclear-capable USSR or the People's Republic of China (known as Red China)—our ideological rivals at the time. When the USSR invaded Afghanistan and USSR-backed Middle Eastern countries attacked US ally Israel, America did not directly intervene with military forces. However, in the last thirty-five years, America has participated in or initiated military action against non-nuclear-capable countries such as Iraq, Iran (1980s failed hostage rescue attempt), Grenada, Panama, the Balkans, Libya (bombing only), Somalia, Lebanon, and Afghanistan. America also deployed military forces to non-nuclear-capable Haiti for humanitarian and peacekeeping reasons.

As an exception, America executed surgical drone attacks and conducted a raid that killed Osama bin Laden in nuclear-capable Pakistan. As another exception, America threatened the use of military force against nuclear-capable USSR and Cuba during the Cold War. President Kennedy drew a nuclear line in the sand during the 1962 Cuban Missile Crisis, when the USSR deployed tactical nuclear missiles in Cuba in response to the US deployment of nuclear missiles in Turkey. In addition to initiating a naval quarantine (euphemism for blockade) of Cuba to prevent the USSR's continued delivery of nuclear missiles and threatening to invade Cuba if the missiles were not dismantled, Kennedy made this chilling statement while addressing the nation: "It shall be the policy of this nation to regard any nuclear missile launched from Cuba against any nation in the Western Hemisphere as an attack by the Soviet Union on the United States, requiring a full retaliatory response upon the Soviet Union" (*Prologue Magazine* 2002).

The USSR fortunately backed down, and since then America has avoided direct military action against a country that has or is suspected to have *deliverable* nuclear weapons. This prompts an interesting question, especially in light of current international tensions regarding Iran's and North Korea's nuclear programs. Since the Cuban Missile Crisis, is America a bully who only picks on non-nuclear-capable nations?

Finally, at the risk of redundancy and overstating my point, compare the Cold War with the current tensions between Iran and Israel/the US when Iranian President Ahmadinejad suggested that US ally Israel should be wiped off the face of the earth. Are Ahmadinejad's comments any different than the saber rattling that existed during the Cold War, when USSR Premier Khrushchev threatened that capitalism (referencing America) would be buried and President Reagan called the USSR an "evil empire" and stated that Marxism and Leninism would end up on the "ash heap of history" ("Ash Heap of History")?

With the above background and for the purposes of this discussion, "bully" is defined as a country that uses superior strength or influence to intimidate or attack a weaker country in order to bend it to the aggressor's geopolitical will. Let's look at Iran and North Korea. They are doppelgangers in their respective development of nuclear technology, with North Korea slightly ahead with confirmed nuclear weapons, albeit without a nuclear missile delivery capability—yet. Iran is suspected of trying to develop nuclear weapons. America has reacted to both countries with diplomatic initiatives and economic sanctions without the application of military force—so far. By comparison, America unilaterally invaded non-nuclear-capable Iraq because of faulty intelligence that indicated it possessed chemical and biological WMDs. Would America have invaded Iraq if it had or was suspected to have nuclear weapons? I think not. Again, does this make America a bully?

On a different note, Israel, India, and Pakistan are not signatories to the Nuclear Proliferation Treaty and possess deliverable nuclear weapons, yet America's response to their nuclear capabilities has been to turn a blind eye because they are allies or friends of America. In 2012, India tested a long-range ballistic missile, and America's reaction was muted to none. Iran and North Korea tested various missiles and North Korea conducted an underground atomic weapon test, and America's reactions were to issue immediate and profuse objections and concerns. Additionally, keep in mind that America deployed Jupiter nuclear missiles on the USSR's border in Turkey but threatened military action when the USSR responded in kind in Cuba during the Cuban Missile Crisis. Is this blatant hypocrisy on America's part?

I believe in a strong military, and if American territory, citizens, or allies are attacked, I support an immediate and overwhelming military response; however, I also expect consistency in the application of military force under all other circumstances. As noted, America's recent history suggests a troubling inconsistency regarding the use of force, all apparently centered on an understandable fear of potential deployments of nuclear weapons. After all, bullies avoid confronting individuals that have the capability or friends with the capability to fight back. With this understanding, it should not be surprising that Iran and North Korea are striving to produce or have produced nuclear weapons.

Two iconic military strategists, Sun Tzu and Karl von Clausewitz, advocated the use of force or going to war *as a last resort*. Again, America seems to adhere to this principle when in conflict with nuclear-capable countries, yet readily threatens or resorts to force with non-nuclear-capable countries in order to impose America's will. As previously mentioned, Iran has operational nuclear reactors, but has yet to develop a nuclear weapon—so far. Nuclear-capable Israel and America have threatened the possibility of military action to stop Iran from developing nuclear weapons. Is Iran another corroborating example of bullying against a non-nuclear-capable country, and is the threatened use of force truly the last resort? Again, if Iran had deliverable nuclear weapons, and with the exception of retaliating if Iran attacked Israel, would America threaten Iran with force? America's historical pattern suggests we would not.

As a peripheral side note, with the exceptions of Grenada, Bosnia, and Panama, American post-Vietnam military intervention has been limited to nonnuclear countries where the predominant religion is Islam. Is this a coincidence or, at the extreme, the birth of a modern-day version of the Holy Crusades?

Von Clausewitz once wrote, "War is a continuation of politics by other means" ("Karl von Clausewitz Quotes"). War can also be a continuation of racism and religious intolerance by other means. And, if the use of military force is the last resort, it must be applied consistently, or America and democracy will lose its moral standing throughout the world. Before America decides to use force, the advice of Sun Tzu would be very appropriate. "For to win one hundred victories in one hundred battles is not the acme of skill," he writes. "To subdue the enemy without fighting is the acme of skill" ("Sun Tzu").

Conflicts

Since the end of the Vietnam War, America has engaged in several short-term military conflicts in Panama, Grenada, Somalia, the Balkans, and Iraq (Operation Desert Storm). However, since 9/11, America has been embroiled in longer-term military operations in Afghanistan and Iraq that have raised questions about America's policies regarding the use of military force in current and future conflicts, the latter focusing on potential hotspots such as Iran and North Korea. The following is my assessment.

Recent: Afghanistan and Iraq

It was learned that Osama bin Laden was the catalyst behind the 9/11 attack and under the protection of the Taliban in Afghanistan. When the Taliban refused to surrender Osama bin Laden and end support for al-Qaeda, America invaded Afghanistan. As stated by President G. W. Bush nine days after 9/11, "Whether we bring our enemies to justice or bring justice to our enemies, justice will be done" (The Quotations Page).

While referring to the eventual killing of Osama bin Laden by SEAL Team Six, Vice President Biden echoed President Bush with a statement that sent an emphatic and unambiguous message to America's enemies: "Those warriors sent a message to the world that if you harm America, we will follow you to the end of the earth" (Rojas 2012).

President Bush then unexpectedly diverted America's attention from Afghanistan by invading Iraq. The legality of Operation Iraqi Freedom is still an issue of continuing debate, especially since the invasion and the subsequent occupation resulted in 4,440-plus soldiers killed in action. This debate has revolved around two main issues.

First, America invaded a sovereign country that had not attacked America or our allies. Historically, there has usually been an act of war against America or one of our allies or a formal declaration of war that preceded major US military action. This was not the case with Operation Iraqi Freedom. Since Operation Desert Storm, Iraq had taken no overt military action or committed an act of war against America or any of America's allies. Granted, there was credible evidence that Iraq had planned to assassinate President H. W. Bush with a car bomb, but the attempt never occurred. Attacking a country's head of state is an act of war; however, planning but not executing such an attack is not an act of war. When the assassination attempt became known, President Clinton ordered a cruise missile attack on Iraq, but did not invade.

Second, America unilaterally invaded Iraq without a United Nations mandate. In 2004, then–UN Secretary-General Kofi Annan was very clear with his objections to Operation Iraqi Freedom, saying, "I have indicated it was not in conformity with the UN Charter. From our point of view, from the charter point of view, it was illegal" ("United Nations Security Council and the Iraq War").

President Bush's rationale for invading Iraq was based on intelligence indicating the possession of WMDs and the alleged presence of al-Qaeda in Iraq, and there was speculation that Iraq was involved in the 9/11 attack—allegations that were eventually proved false. This led to charges that the Bush Administration fabricated evidence to justify an invasion he had planned to launch anyway. There was even speculation that Bush acted out of revenge for Iraq's assassination plan against his father. Anything is possible, but I do not believe these allegations. I believe the grievous breakdown in the US intelligence apparatus resulted in an ill-advised rush to judgment such that the invasion of Iraq was a foregone conclusion.

My beliefs are corroborated by former Secretary of State Colin Powell in his book, *It Worked for Me: In Life and Leadership*. Powell states there was never a formal debate about whether invading Iraq was a good idea. Powell's assertion is echoed by former CIA Director George Tenet. An analysis of national security archives in 2010 concluded that there was no record that Bush made a studied decision for war. White House and Pentagon meetings focused on moving the war planning forward, not whether invading Iraq was a proper course of action for America and its allies (Dan Froomkin 2012).

As another point of debate, Iraq had WMDs during Operation Desert Storm and did not use them. There were very defensible reasons to invade Iraq during Operation Desert Storm, but the scope of the UN mandate did not allow for such an action. If America did not unilaterally invade Iraq when it was proven they had WMDs, why use WMDs as an excuse to invade Iraq over a decade later?

President Bush finally admitted that Iraq did not have WMDs and had no involvement with 9/11. With this admission, it could be argued that he was guilty of a gross lack of judgment and failure in leadership. I am reminded of an extract of the epic 1854 poem "The Charge of the Light Brigade" by Sir Alfred Lord Tennyson.

> All in the valley of Death
> Rode the six hundred . . .
>
> Forward, the Light Brigade!
> Was there a man dismayed?
> Not tho' the soldier knew
> Someone had blundered.
> Theirs not to make reply,
> Theirs not to reason why,
> Theirs but to do and die . . .

Into Iraq rode the 4,440-plus soldiers who did not ask why and died because of President G. W. Bush's decision to invade Iraq. A disabled and dying Iraqi war veteran wrote an emotional letter to President Bush and former Vice President Cheney on the tenth anniversary of Operation Iraqi Freedom. "The Iraq War is the largest strategic blunder in US history," he wrote. "On every level—moral, strategic, military, and economic—Iraq was a failure. And it was you, Mr. Bush and Mr. Cheney, who started this war. It is you who should pay the consequences" (Young 2013).

The Future: Iran, North Korea, or Elsewhere?

As previously discussed, there is mounting international tension regarding Iran's nuclear program, and North Korea recently threatened military action against Japan, US bases, and South Korea. The Iranian and North Korean issues are being addressed diplomatically, along with the imposition of crippling international economic sanctions. These sanctions are reminiscent of those levied against Japan that prompted Japan to attack America at Pearl Harbor, resulting in a formal declaration of war against Japan and America's entrance into WWII. Again, those who fail to learn from history are doomed to repeat it. America must proceed very carefully with Iran and North Korea because the most passive of animals will strike back if trapped into a corner, as was the case with Japan.

Granted, Iran is a noncompliant party to the Nuclear Proliferation Treaty, but would their fledgling nuclear program be a valid reason for military action? The threat to Israel is palpable and Iran's connection to terrorism undeniable; however, in contrast, America has not attacked North Korea, who has confirmed nuclear weapons, repeatedly threatened our allies (Japan and South Korea) and US military bases, has suspected ties to international smuggling, and withdrew as a party from the Nuclear Proliferation Treaty ("Treaty on the Non-Proliferation of Nuclear Weapons").

I do not have a solution for the Iranian or North Korean problems. I hope diplomacy works, but if military action is necessary, as would be the case if North Korea followed through with its threats, Leon Trotsky's advice is worth remembering: "Where force is necessary, there it must be applied boldly, decisively and completely. But one must know the limitations of force; one must know when to blend force with a maneuver, a blow with an agreement" ("Quotes About Force").

I hope America keeps this advice in mind while evaluating the possibility of military action in a new Middle East hotspot—Syria—a discussion for another time.

Drone Attacks

Technologies such as the Global Positioning System and other space-related technologies; smart bombs, artillery shells, and missiles; weaponized and nonweaponized drones; stealth aircraft and ships; night vision and targeting capabilities; and computers have taken prominent roles in the conduct of war over the last forty years. The rules of warfare have changed to be consistent with and govern the use of these technologies. One such set of rules are the Rules of Engagement (ROE). The ROE determine the circumstances and manner in which military force may be applied. For example, US Army radar sites would set up along suspected North Korean infiltration routes in the Korean Demilitarized Zone. The ROE mandated that radar sites be positioned such that the radar beam did not cross the North Korean border. Also keep in mind the care that soldiers fighting in Afghanistan had to exercise to ensure they did not fire into neighboring Pakistan.

Regarding the possibility of civilian casualties, President Obama authorized a very debatable ROE allowing for the collateral death of military-aged males who are in the proximity of drone-targeted terrorists. I concur with using drones in the fight against terrorism, but I have problems with the potential application of this new policy if it is based on this flawed logic:

> It in effect counts all military-age males in a strike zone as combatants, according to several administration officials, unless there is explicit intelligence posthumously proving them innocent . . . Counterterrorism officials insist this approach is one of simple logic: people in an area of known terrorist activity, or found with a top Qaeda operative, are probably up to no good. (Balko 2012)

For the sake of argument, what about adding women to this protocol? Being an illegal combatant or terrorist is not the exclusive domain of males, as has already been proven by female suicide bombers, such as the Black Widows in Chechnya; here is where the moral dilemma begins. Are children next? After all, there are children who have been impressed into the armed service of various rebel and criminal factions in places such as Africa, and children are being used as couriers of improvised explosive devices for al-Qaeda terrorists. In other words, where is the moral line drawn or, more ominously, is the line disappearing?

As another factor to consider, the US Department of Justice wrote a whitepaper that concluded it was legal for American citizens to be attacked and killed by drone attacks on foreign soil if they cannot be captured and presented an imminent danger, even if they are not engaged in combative activities at the time of the attack—all without due process or judicial review. As of May 2013, four Americans have been killed by drone attacks on foreign soil. Additionally, the DOJ made a determination that the president of the United States has the legal authority to order similar drone attacks against US citizens on American soil; however, President Obama stated this would only occur under "extraordinary circumstances." I am comfortable with his assurance, but America must be careful not to start sliding down another slippery slope, first killing military-aged males abroad and then American citizens abroad and at home. Who will be next?

Even though the realities of war result in civilian collateral damage, America must be extremely sensitive to the potential alienation of the population whose hearts and minds we are trying to win. The continued killing of innocent civilians will only harden sentiments against America and produce a fertile pool of recruits for the terrorists. Ironically, even Osama bin Laden understood this concept. Fearing Muslim backlash against al-Qaeda for the mounting numbers of civilian Muslim deaths, he urged al-Qaeda operatives to avoid killing innocent Muslims during attacks (YouTube 2012).

Consider the advice Arnaud Amalric, a Catholic cleric, gave to a Holy Crusader who was struggling with distinguishing friend from foe during a battle in 1209. "Kill them all," he said. "For the Lord knows them that are His" ("Arnaud Amalric"). Or, as restated during the Vietnam War, "Kill them all and let God sort it out" (author unknown).

On a parallel note, when asked what he thought about forgiving those who harbored and abetted the 9/11 terrorists, the late US Army General H. Norman Schwarzkopf Jr. reportedly replied, "I believe that forgiving them is God's function. Our [military] job is simply to arrange the meeting" ("Gen. H. Norman Schwarzkopf").

I agree with General Schwarzkopf's sentiments, but I still take issue with targeting illegal combatants and terrorists without regard for the possibility of collateral civilian deaths because association does not automatically mean guilt. As a rule, military snipers will not shoot if the targeted individual is not carrying a weapon or cannot be positively identified as a combatant or terrorist, or if there is a risk of hitting nearby innocent civilians. Why should drone attacks be handled any differently? Unless individuals are holding weapons, caught in the act of burying IEDs, or similar actions, a definitive friend-or-foe distinction from a drone video feed cannot be made because most illegal combatants and terrorists do not wear uniforms. There is a legal principle that it is better to let ten guilty people go free than to convict or execute one innocent person. Should one illegal combatant or terrorist be allowed to go free to prevent the deaths of ten civilians who cannot be conclusively identified as illegal combatants or terrorists?

Again, the war on terror is unconventional and not a formally declared war against a sovereign country with uniformed armed forces. This changes the ROE, requiring increased diligence and restraint prior to initiating deadly force. I understand that war is hell, but just because terrorists have no regard for innocent civilian lives, is it right for America to act in a similar manner? With President Obama's drone policy, does America risk becoming the very terrorists we are trying to eliminate?

On an historical note, the strategic carpet-bombing of cities in Germany and Japan resulted in one million-plus civilian deaths during WWII. Granted, a formal state of war existed, but from a moral perspective, was it right? Former Air Force Chief of Staff Curtis LeMay and former Secretary of Defense Robert McNamara (a Lieutenant Colonel under General LeMay's command during WWII) postulated that if the US had lost the war against Japan, they both would have been tried and convicted of war crimes for the fire-bombing of Japanese cities (McNamara, *The Fog of War* 2003).

Technologies that protect soldiers from injury or death are crucial to success; however, even though lives are saved by placing technology instead of soldiers in harm's way, drones and similar technologies desensitize warfare. Combat pilots admit that it is much easier to drop bombs on combatants whose faces they cannot see as compared to front-line soldiers who have to kill combatants who can be seen up close and personal through rifle scopes, or during close-quarters and hand-to-hand combat. In my opinion, President Obama's current policies embrace the dehumanizing aspects of technology in warfare, thus making the decision to take noncombatant lives as easy as pressing a key on a computer keyboard.

Technology allows us to think of our enemies as mere data on a hard drive, suppressing our sense of humanity. In our zeal to destroy our enemies, the resulting lack of moral restraint provides a convenient justification for the indiscriminate taking of civilian lives. America's intent to defend its people and territory is the primary mission of the commander in chief and the military; however, if we are not careful, America could lose its moral standing by reducing the value of human life to nothing more than soulless avatars on a video screen. To his credit, President Obama has since indicated a possible change of heart regarding these issues.

On May 23, 2013, President Obama said that since the death of Osama bin Laden and most of his top lieutenants, and since there had been no large-scale terrorist attacks on American soil, and due to the increasing number of civilian casualties from drone attacks, a new counter-terrorism policy was warranted that would include limiting drone strikes and a shift toward capturing rather than killing terrorist suspects. Regarding this shift in policy, President Obama cautioned:

> We must define the nature and scope of this struggle, or else it will define us . . . To say a military tactic is legal, or even effective, is not to say it is wise or moral in every instance, for the same progress that gives us the technology to strike half a world away also demands the discipline to constrain that power, or risk abusing it. (*Washington Post* 2013)

Hopefully, President Obama's words translate into actual policy and execution.

Order and Discipline

The maintenance of good military order and discipline is required of every US military service member; however, breakdowns do occur, such as breaking the faith and sexual abuse. If uncorrected, these egregious behaviors could erode the military's cohesiveness, morale, and combat effectiveness.

Breaking the Faith

The leaking of classified or sensitive military, intelligence, and diplomatic information must stop. These leaks have emanated from a variety of sources, but the leaking of such information by fellow veterans is most disheartening because they broke the faith. Breaking the faith involves any action that brings discredit upon the uniform, the current or former unit, the chain of command, or America—whether on active duty or not. This also includes actions that break the unwritten rules regarding confidentiality and discretion, protecting the safety and well-being of comrades-in-arms, and never leaving a comrade behind on the battlefield. Recently, active-duty and former Navy SEALS broke the faith by allegedly disclosing sensitive military information and closely held operational procedures for financial gain and public celebrity.

Most notably, a former SEAL Team Six member, who participated in the raid that killed Osama bin Laden, wrote about the raid in the book *No Easy Day*. In violation of protocol, this book was not submitted for vetting by the Pentagon or intelligence community prior to publication. Additionally, such disclosures egregiously violated very important expectations everyone in the military, especially special operations "operators," have of each other—trust and honor. The head of the Naval Special Warfare Command at that time, Navy Rear Admiral Sean Pybus, wrote a pointed letter to all Navy SEALs and associated support personnel that read, in part:

> I am disappointed, embarrassed, and concerned. Most of us have always thought that the privilege of working with some of our nation's toughest warriors on challenging missions would be enough to be proud of, with no further compensation

or celebrity required. Today, we find former SEALs headlining positions in a presidential campaign, hawking details about a mission against Enemy Number One [Osama bin Laden] and generally selling other aspects of NSW training and operations. For an elite force that should be humble and disciplined for life, we are certainly not appearing to be so. We owe our chain of command much better than this. (Starr 2012)

To the extent that any disclosures involved classified or otherwise sensitive information that violated the law or nondisclosure agreements, violators should be prosecuted to the fullest extent of the law. If disclosures do not violate the law or nondisclosure agreements but still break the faith, the violator should be excommunicated from and shunned by the military community that was dishonored. In other words, with the exception of acknowledging his or her active-duty service in official military records, the violator should no longer be recognized within the military community. It has come to my attention that this is exactly how the author of *No Easy Day* is currently being treated by the Navy SEAL community—most appropriate.

Sexual Abuse

Sexual abuse in the military will be discussed with the disclaimer that I have been retired from the military for twenty years. My comments will be based on the culture I experienced prior to my retirement as a field-grade officer. Before I start, I must first state that I totally support the US military; however, sexual abuse must be eradicated from its midst.

Over time, critics have labeled the military as anachronistic, elitist, racist, or sexist. The military may have earned these descriptors at various times throughout its history, but one thing has always been a constant paradigm—"duty, honor, country." This paradigm was eloquently presented by General Douglas MacArthur during a 1962 speech at West Point.

For all hours and for all time, it is an expression of the ethics of the American soldier . . . Duty, honor, country: Those three hallowed words reverently dictate what you ought to be, what you can be, what you will be. They are your rallying point to build courage when courage seems to fail, to regain faith when there seems to be little cause for faith, to create hope when hope becomes forlorn. (Suiter 2011)

This is the military I knew and assume is still the same today. In accordance with this belief, I will approach sexual abuse from the perspective of removing rotten apples from an otherwise honorable military barrel—not from the perspective that the barrel is also rotten.

Again, sexual abuse has no place in the military or American society. It is illegal, abhorrent, a betrayal of and dishonor to the uniform, and contrary to good military order and discipline. Sexual abuse also breaks the faith, a component of which is a long-standing principle that service members, as brothers and sisters, will always protect each other's back—a protection that unfortunately has not been extended to all men and women in the military.

Regarding sexual abuse against female service members, one of the catalysts sparking the eruption of incidents may have been the integration of women into previously all-male bastions of the military elite, such as combat pilots, navy submariners, and US service academy cadets. This integration culminated with the directive from former Secretary of Defense Leon Panetta in 2013 to integrate women into all combat units throughout the military to include special operations units. Since the start of this integration decades ago, reactions were and still are mixed and, at its worst, malicious and retaliatory. This could be one the causes for the increase in the number of sexual harassment and abuse incidents toward female service members.

On a purely speculative note, even though there is no excuse for sexual abuse under any circumstances, could another catalyst be the extended combat and social isolation in Afghanistan and Iraq since 9/11? The incidents of post-traumatic stress disorder and suicide among active-duty and former service members are growing concerns. It should also be noted that, in 2012, more than eighty-five thousand veterans were treated for injuries or illness stemming from sexual abuse in the military (Associated Press 2013).

Before continuing, it is important to understand the principle of accountability in the military. Noncommissioned officers (NCO) are held to very high standards of leadership; however, these standards are at their highest for warrant and commissioned officers, especially officers in command positions. A commander is ultimately held accountable for everything that happens within his or her command. For example, if soldiers suffer frostbite or heat-related injuries during training exercises, depending on the circumstances of the injuries, the soldiers' leader can be held accountable and face the possibility of being relieved of duty or other forms of nonjudicial punishment for not assuring the welfare and safety of the soldiers under his or her command or supervision. This is an instant career killer if such punishment is permanently recorded in the officer's or NCO's personnel file.

Additionally, the military's official doctrine of command responsibility holds commanders accountable if they become aware of violations of the United States Code of Military Justice, the Geneva Convention, war crimes, or anything contrary to maintaining good order and discipline without appropriate action. Such has occurred during the Abu Ghraib prisoner abuse scandal in Iraq, the My Lai massacre during the Vietnam War, and the Tailhook sexual abuse scandal in Las Vegas, Nevada. This rigid doctrine and its potential impact on an officer's career may be contributing factors to a commander's reluctance to report and act on the sexual abuse of soldiers under his or her command, even to the extent of discouraging or coercing sex abuse victims from officially submitting complaints or attacking the veracity of submitted complaints in the same manner that a defense attorney attacks the character of a rape victim in an attempt to deflect attention away from the defendant.

Lastly, if service members have a complaint and feel that they did not receive justice from their chain of command, there is the option to escalate complaints to the Inspector General (IG). However, there is an unwritten rule that officers do not go to the IG with complaints. Doing so could have painful career consequences, and many female officers do not report sexual abuse incidents to their chain of command for fear of being ostracized or having their performance evaluations "tweaked" such that the evaluations are no longer competitive with their peers—a lose-lose situation. In other words, an officer's sexual abuse complaint to the chain of command or IG may be acted upon, but at the risk of an officer's career—a Pyrrhic victory. This may be why some female officers resign their commissions rather than continually tiptoeing through professionally and emotionally tenuous minefields. Female enlisted service members also leave the military for similar reasons.

The similarity between the Catholic Church's pedophilia and the military's sexual abuse scandals are striking. They both initially closed ranks in order to protect their respective hierarchies and avoid public backlash and official investigations. Regarding the military, after the 1991 Tailhook scandal in which eighty-three male and female officers were sexually abused by US Navy and Marine pilots, only low-level officers were disciplined. Not one general officer was disciplined, even though some in attendance were allegedly aware of the abuses as they occurred ("Tailhook Scandal"). It is now the year 2013, and the Catholic Church and military are coming to grips with the realities of pedophilia and sexual abuse, respectively. In the military, service members of all ranks are being disciplined for sexually inappropriate behaviors, and commanders are being held accountable for the inappropriate behaviors of service members under their command. For example, the commanding general of US Army forces in Japan, Major General Michael Harrison, was relieved of command for failing to properly investigate a sexual assault allegation (Burns 2013). This is a good start, but more needs to be done, especially at the highest levels in the military.

Female officers are still struggling to shatter glass ceilings. It took until the 1970s for a woman to be promoted to the rank of one-star general, and 2008 for the first to be promoted to the highest rank of four-star general—ranks that have the power to influence military culture. In 2009, there were close to a thousand general officers in the military, yet less than a hundred were women (Meyer). This is the same arduous battle female managers are fighting in corporate America to achieve executive-level positions. Until more women are promoted to general officer ranks and assigned as commanders of major commands, and until service members start defending their comrades from sexual abuse and report all incidents, sexual abuse will continue to tarnish the military's reputation and legacy.

An appropriate end to this discussion would be to ask one simple question of all military service members. Would you stand idly by while a blood family member was being sexually abused? Need more be said?

EPILOGUE

> God grant me the serenity to accept the things I cannot change, courage to change the things I can, and wisdom to know the difference.—Reinhold Niebuhr (Niebuhr 1943)

I am a citizen of the greatest country in the world, but America can be greater. My concerns reflect an ardent desire for America to continue on a path to true greatness, but in my opinion, changes are needed, and change starts with the American citizen.

America is struggling with a wounded but healing spirit, a suffering but slowly recovering economy, and a very divisive government. A generation of young Americans is growing up without a work ethic while expecting entitlements and handouts, or conversely, not able to find jobs due to a high unemployment rate. The American Dream has become a windfall for the rich and a very expensive proposition for the poor, disenfranchised, and shrinking middle class, all making me wonder, "How do I feel about my country? And how does my country feel about me? Are we only to be Americans when the mood suits you?" (Braugher 1995).

I will continue to ask these questions until we the people do something to snap America out of this lingering malaise. If we do not speak up and act, Martin Niemöller's epiphany regarding not speaking out against Nazi Germany may apply to Americans:

> First they came for the Socialists, and I did not speak out because I was not a Socialist. Then they came for the Trade Unionists, and I did not speak out because I was not a Trade Unionist. Then they came for the Jews, and I did not speak out because I was not a Jew. Then they came for me, and there was no one left to speak for me. (United States Holocaust Memorial Museum)

I am not comparing America to Nazi Germany. Niemöller's comments are a reminder of what *could* happen if citizens did not vote, petition for redress of grievances, or most importantly, ensure "that government of the people, by the people, for the people, shall not perish from the earth." And, to all Americans who play it safe by not speaking out, I offer this challenge: "Life should not be a journey to the grave with the intention of arriving safely in a pretty and well-preserved body, but rather to skid in broadside in a cloud of smoke, thoroughly used up, totally worn out, and loudly proclaiming, 'Wow! What a *ride!*'" (Thompson).

I wrote *We the Who?* while skidding "in broadside in a cloud of smoke," without professional or academic-level research or access to the inner workings of government or subject matter experts. However, at the end of my skid, my body of knowledge evolved, reinforcing or amending beliefs I had before I started writing *We the Who?*. In short, I have become a more informed American citizen. Asking questions, probing, expressing opinions, and holding elected leaders accountable to keep us informed so we can make quality decisions about our lives will reduce the lack of understanding and frustration that I believe currently exists among many Americans.

Whether you agree with my thinking or believe I am totally out to lunch, I hope I made you think and prompted you to ask questions. *Our constitutional right to do so without reprisal makes America great.* After all, who are we as Americans if we do not express and stand up for what we believe?

America has become a more perfect union, but it is not perfect. America will have problems, but they will be solved. Americans will have disagreements, but they will be resolved. Americans may be of many colors and cultures, have diverse beliefs and opinions, and may be rich, poor, or somewhere in between, but when it counts, Americans will *always* be united as one—as we the people—even when we sometimes ask, "We the who?"

On this note, I will leave you—for now—and wish you a long and fruitful life, liberty, and success in your pursuit of happiness.

BIBLIOGRAPHY

100% Compensation. *Personal Injury Compensation Awards in the UK.* n.d. http://www.100percent-compensation.co.uk/compensation_awards. htm (accessed February 24, 2012).

ACLU. *Illegal Detentions in the "War on Terror."* n.d. http://www.aclu. org/indefinitedetention/ (accessed February 21, 2012).

ADL: Anti-Defamation League. *Separation: Good for Government, Good for Religion.* n.d. http://www.adl.org/issue_religious_freedom/ separation_cs_primer.asp (accessed February 25, 2012).

Advertisement Journal. *Television Networks Irresponsible, Insensitive: Kids Don't Need Cameras Thrust In Their Faces, At Such Traumatic Times.* 15 December 2012. http://www.advertisementjournal.com/2012/12/ television-networks-irresponsible-insensitive-kids-dont-need-cameras-thrust-in-their-faces-at-such-traumatic-times/ (accessed March 23, 2013).

The American President. Directed by Rob Reiner. Performed by Michael Douglas. 1995.

Associated Press. *More than 85,000 veterans treated last year over alleged military sex abuse, report says.* 20 May 2013. http://www.foxnews. com/us/2013/05/20/more-than-85000-veterans-treated-last-year-over-alleged-military-sex-abuse/ (accessed May 24, 2013).

———. *US government records $116.5 billion surplus in June.* 11 July 2013. http://www.foxnews.com/politics/2013/07/11/us-government-records-1165-billion-surplus-in-june/ (accessed July 2013, 2013).

Associated Press and the Huffington Post. *Joe Biden 'Chains' Remark Seized Upon By Mitt Romney's Campaign.* 15 August 2012. http://www. huffingtonpost.com/2012/08/14/joe-biden-chains-remark_n_1776463. html (accessed August 15, 2012).

Balko, Radley. *U.S. Drone Policy: Standing Near Terrorists Makes You A Terrorist.* 28 May 2012. http://www.huffingtonpost.com/2012/05/29/ drone-attacks-innocent-civilians_n_1554380.html (accessed May 30, 2012).

Bartleby.com. *Abraham Lincoln Second Inaugural Address.* 1989. http:// www.bartleby.com/124/pres32.html (accessed June 22, 2013).

Bassett, Laura. *Lila Rose: Beatriz Doesn't Need A Life-Saving Abortion.* 31 May 2013. http://www.huffingtonpost.com/2013/05/31/lila-rose-beatriz-abortion_n_3367595.html (accessed May 31, 2013).

BBC. *Abortion.* 7 September 2009. http://www.bbc.co.uk/religion/religions/islam/islamethics/abortion_1.shtml (accessed April 9, 2013).

Bible Gateway. *1 Samuel 15:3 (English Standard Version).* n.d. http://www.biblegateway.com/passage/?search=1%20Samuel%2015:3%20&version=ESV (accessed April 3, 2013).

———. *John 8:7 (King James Version).* n.d. http://www.biblegateway.com/passage/?search=John+8%3A7&version=KJV (accessed March 24, 2013).

———. *John 8:11 (King James Version).* n.d. http://www.biblegateway.com/passage/?search=John+8%3A11&version=KJV (accessed June 29, 2013).

———. *Mark 8:36 (King James Version).* n.d. http://www.biblegateway.com/passage/?search=Mark+8%3A36&version=KJV (accessed April 15, 2013).

———. *Psalms 137:9. (English Standard Version).* n.d. http://www.biblegateway.com/passage/?search=Psalms%20137:%209&version=ESV (accessed April 8, 2013).

———. *Romans 12:19 (King James Version).* n.d. http://www.biblegateway.com/passage/?search=Romans+12%3A19&version=KJV (accessed March 24, 2013).

Black Americans in Congress. *Historical Data.* n.d. http://baic.house.gov/historical-data/congressional-committee-chairs.html (accessed July 4, 2012).

Bloomberg, Michael. *Compass Quotes.* n.d. http://www.brainyquote.com/quotes/keywords/compass.html (accessed June 24, 2012).

Blumenthal, Paul. *IRS Approved More Conservative Groups Than Liberal Groups Selected For Review: Report.* 6 June 2013. http://www.huffingtonpost.com/2013/06/06/irs-conservative-groups_n_3396998.html (accessed June 6, 2013).

Bornstein, Brian H. and Edie Greene. "Determining Damages: The Psychology of Jury Awards." *The American Psychological Association.* 2003. http://www.bsos.umd.edu/gvpt/lpbr/subpages/reviews/greene-bornstein305.htm (accessed February 24, 2012).

Botelho, Greg. *Saved by Jewish man on 9/11, Pakistani Muslim reaches out.* 2 September 2002. http://archives.cnn.com/2002/US/08/30/ar911.usman.farman/index.html (accessed April 16, 2013).

BrainyQuote. *Albert Einstein Quotes.* n.d. http://www.brainyquote.com/quotes/quotes/a/alberteins386089.html (accessed May 28, 2012).

———. *Douglas MacArthur Quotes.* n.d. http://www.brainyquote.com/quotes/quotes/d/douglasmac125212.html (accessed July 21, 2012).

———. *Eleanor Roosevelt Quotes.* n.d. http://www.brainyquote.com/quotes/authors/e/eleanor_roosevelt.html (accessed July 24, 2012).

———. *Karl Von Clausewitz Quotes.* n.d. http://www.brainyquote.com/quotes/authors/k/karl_von_clausewitz.html (accessed September 19, 2012).

———. *Ron Paul Quotes.* n.d. http://www.brainyquote.com/quotes/quotes/r/ronpaul173223.html (accessed September 23, 2012).

Burns, Robert. *Major General Michael T. Harrison Suspended By Army For Allegedly Mishandling Sexual Assault Case.* 7 June 2013. http://www.huffingtonpost.com/2013/06/07/major-general-michael-harrison-suspended_n_3406246.html (accessed June 8, 2013).

Burton, Nsenga. *It's a Great Time to Be Racist.* 12 August 2011. http://www.theroot.com/views/its-great-time-be-racist (accessed February 28, 2012).

Cafferty, Jack. *Should President Obama have apologized for the inadvertent burning of Qurans?* 28 February 2012. http://caffertyfile.blogs.cnn.com/2012/02/28/should-president-obama-have-apologized-for-the-inadvertent-burning-of-qurans/ (accessed August 1, 2012).

Caldwell, Alicia A. *Undocumented Immigrant Releases Acknowledged By John Morton Of Homeland Security Department.* 14 March 2013. http://www.huffingtonpost.com/2013/03/14/undocumented-immigrant-releases_n_2875900.html (accessed March 14, 2013).

Catspirit. *Famous Flip Floppers—Candidates who Change their Mind—Historically, not a 'Bad Thing.'* 12 January 2012. http://www.allvoices.com/contributed-news/11286105/content/89569681-famous-flip-floppers?window_location=503 (accessed September 7, 2012).

CBS News. *Politics.* 27 January 2010. http://www.cbsnews.com/2100-504643_162-6146723.html (accessed February 26, 2012).

Cesca, Bob. *Republicans Filibuster Everything, Romney Blames Obama for Not Working With Congress.* 25 October 2012. http://www.

huffingtonpost.com/bob-cesca/republicans-filibuster-ev_b_2018663.
html (accessed October 27, 2012).

The Charters of Freedom. *Bill of Rights.* n.d. http://www.archives.gov/
exhibits/charters/bill_of_rights_transcript.html (accessed July 22,
2012).

———. "Constitution of the United States." *The Charters of Freedom.*
n.d. http://www.archives.gov/exhibits/charters/constitution_transcript.
html (accessed August 5, 2012).

Chicago Police Department. *2011 Chicago Murder Analysis.* 6 January 2012.
https://portal.chicagopolice.org/portal/page/portal/ClearPath/News/
Statistical%20Reports/Murder%20Reports/MA11.pdf (accessed January
20, 2013).

Chrish. *"Truth in Campaigning" overturned.* 13 October 2005. http://
www.newshounds.us/2005/10/13/truth_in_campaigning_overturned.
php (accessed March 15, 2012).

CNN. *Newsroom.* Television. 24 October 2012.

CNN Money. *Divorce duel reveals Welch's perks.* 6 September 2002.
http://money.cnn.com/2002/09/06/news/companies/welch_ge/
(accessed March 5, 2012).

Coates, Ta-Nehisi. *Fear of a Black President.* 28 August 2012. http://
www.theatlantic.com/magazine/archive/2012/09/fear-of-a-black-
president/309064/ (accessed August 28, 2012).

Coffina, Scott. *Gun Control by Executive Order.* 16 January 2013. http://
www.nationalreview.com/articles/337789/gun-control-executive-
order-scott-coffina?pg=1 (accessed January 21, 2013).

Cohen, Tom. *Obama administration to stop deporting some young illegal
immigrants.* 16 June 2012. http://www.cnn.com/2012/06/15/politics/
immigration/index.html (accessed September 24, 2012).

Colasurdo, Nancy. *What's With Our Rush to Judgment?* 25 January 2012.
http://www.foxbusiness.com/personal-finance/2012/01/24/whats-
with-our-rush-to-judgment/ (accessed July 22, 2012).

Congressional Research Service. *Criminal Prohibitions on the Publication
of Classified Defense Information.* 31 January 2013. http://www.fas.
org/sgp/crs/secrecy/R41404.pdf (accessed May 23, 2013).

Constitution Society. *The Magna Carta (The Great Chapter).* 11 March
2013. http://www.constitution.org/eng/magnacar.htm (accessed March
19, 2013).

Curtis, Drew. *News Media Quotes.* n.d. http://www.brainyquote.com/quotes/keywords/news_media.html (accessed March 23, 2013).

Dark Girls. Directed by Bill Duke and D. Channsin Berry. 2011.

Democratic Leadership Council. *Keynote Address of Gov. Bill Clinton to the DLC's Cleveland Convention.* 6 May 1991. http://www.dlc.org/ndol_ci0fd7.html?kaid=86&subid=194&contentid=3166 (accessed May 25, 2013).

Democracy Now! News for All the People: Juan González & Joseph Torres on the Epic Story of Race & the U.S. Media. 13 October 2011. http://m.democracynow.org/stories/12257 (accessed April 22, 2013).

Department of Labor. "The Worker Adjustment and Retraining Notification Act." *Department of Labor.* n.d. http://www.doleta.gov/programs/factsht/warn.htm (accessed August 12, 2012).

Department of the Army. In *Field Manual 2-22.3: Human Intelligence Collector Operations,* by Department of the Army, 137, 161–176. Department of the Army, 2006.

DiversityInc. *10 Things Never to Say to a Black Co-Worker.* n.d. http://www.diversityinc.com/things-not-to-say/10-things-never-to-say-to-a-black-coworker/ (accessed October 5, 2012).

DNC2012. *Full text of Bill Clinton's speech at the Democratic National Convention.* 5 September 2012. http://www.charlotteobserver.com/2012/09/05/3507368/full-text-of-bill-clintons-speech.html (accessed September 6, 2012).

Dougherty, Michael. *14 Bald-Faced Mitt Romney Flip-Flops That Were Dug Up By John McCain.* 18 January 2012. http://www.businessinsider.com/14-bald-faced-mitt-romney-flip-flops-that-were-dug-up-by-john-mccain-2012-1?op=1 (accessed September 7, 2012).

Electronic Text Center. *HEARING OF THE SENATE JUDICIARY COMMITTEE ON THE NOMINATION OF CLARENCE THOMAS TO THE SUPREME COURT.* n.d. http://etext.lib.virginia.edu/etcbin/toccer-new-yitna?id=UsaThom&images=images/modeng&data=/lv6/workspace/yitna&tag=public&part=24 (accessed May 8, 2012).

Elk, Mike. *Koch Sends Pro-Romney Mailing to 45,000 Employees While Stifling Workplace Political Speech.* 15 October 2012. http://www.beyondchron.org/news/index.php?itemid=10603 (accessed October 18, 2012).

Elliot, Phillip. *Harry Reid 'Negro' Comment: Reid Apologizes For 'No Negro Dialect' Comment.* 9 January 2010. http://www.huffingtonpost.

com/2010/01/09/harry-reid-negro-comment-_n_417406.html (accessed May 3, 2013).

Examiner.com. *The character assassination of President Obama.* 19 October 2010. http://www.examiner.com/liberal-in-newark/the-character-assassination-of-president-obama (accessed March 15, 2012).

Fabian, Jordan and Yager, Jordy. *The Hill's Blog Briefing Room.* 11 March 2011. http://thehill.com/blogs/blog-briefing-room/news/148643-first-muslim-in-congress-breaks-into-tears-during-radicalization-hearing (accessed February 27, 2012).

Fashionista. *The Changing Face of the All-American Model.* n.d. http://www.stylelist.com/view/the-changing-face-of-the-all-american-model/?icid=maing-grid7%7Cmain5%7Cdl28%7Csec1_lnk3%26pLid%3D341320#!slide=41292 (accessed July 9, 2013).

Finocchiaro, Peter. *Lawrence Wilkerson, Former Colin Powell Aide, Blasts Sununu, GOP, As 'Full Of Racists'.* 26 October 2012. http://www.huffingtonpost.com/2012/10/26/lawrence-wilkerson-colin-powell-sununu_n_2027721.html (accessed October 27, 2012).

Fletcher, Michael A. and Kevin Merida. "Courting Venom." In *Supreme Discomfort: The Divided Soul of Clarence Thomas*, by Kevin Merida and Michael A. Fletcher, 18. New York: Doubleday, 2007.

The Fog of War. Directed by Errol Morris. Performed by Robert McNamara. 2003.

Foley, Elise. *Immigration Enforcement Cost Higher Than FBI, Policing Drugs, Guns Combined: Report.* 7 January 2013. http://www.huffingtonpost.com/2013/01/07/immigration-enforcement-cost_n_2425647.html?ref=topbar (accessed January 25, 2013).

Foster, Stephen D. *In Unprecedented Move, Republicans Refuse To Allow President Obama To Speak Before Joint Session Of Congress.* 21 August 2011. http://www.addictinginfo.org/2011/08/31/in-unprecedented-move-republicans-refuse-to-allow-president-obama-to-speak-before-joint-session-of-congress/ (accessed February 26, 2012).

FoxNews.com. *Bush Apologizes for Iraqi Prisoner Abuse.* 7 March 2004. http://www.foxnews.com/story/0,2933,119156,00.html (accessed August 1, 2012).

———. *NBC issues apology for edited Zimmerman 911 call.* 3 April 2012. http://www.foxnews.com/us/2012/04/03/nbc-issues-apology-edited-zimmerman-11-call/ (accessed July 21, 2012).

Free Advice. *How do insurance companies and juries assign values to pain and suffering? What factors do they take into account?* n.d. http://injury-law.freeadvice.com/injury-law/injury-law/pain_and_suffering_factors.htm (accessed February 24, 2012).

Froomkin, Dan. *Colin Powell's New Book: War With Iraq Never Debated.* 9 May 2012. http://www.huffingtonpost.com/2012/05/09/colin-powell-book_n_1503592.html?icid=maing-grid7%7Cmain5%7Cdl39%7Csec1_lnk1%26pLid%3D159352 (accessed May 9, 2012).

Gallup. *"Pro-Choice" Americans at Record-Low 41%.* 23 May 2012. http://www.gallup.com/poll/154838/Pro-Choice-Americans-Record-Low.aspx (accessed August 22, 2012).

Gentilviso, Chris. *Rush Limbaugh: Obama, Chris Christie Have A 'Master-Servant Relationship.'* 28 May 2013. http://www.huffingtonpost.com/2013/05/28/rush-limbaugh-obama-chris-christie_n_3349891.html (accessed May 29, 2013).

Germano, Roy. *How many illegal immigrants live in the United States and where do they come from?* 18 March 2011. http://roygermano.wordpress.com/2011/03/18/how-many-illegal-immigrants-live-in-the-united-states-and-where-do-they-come-from/ (accessed March 3, 2012).

Google. *Where Was the Manufactured Outrage From the Right When This happened?* Google. n.d. http://ametia.files.wordpress.com/2013/05/bush-with-marines-holding-umbrella1.png (accessed May 20, 2013).

Gordon, Claire. *Utah Employer, Terry Lee Forensics, Fires Workers Supporting Obama.* 18 January 2013. http://jobs.aol.com/articles/2013/01/18/utah-terry-lee-forensics-fires-supporting-obama-two-employees/?icid=maing-grid7%7Cmain5%7Cdl17%7Csec1_lnk1%26pLid%3D259104 (accessed January 19, 2013).

Greene, Edith, Jane Goodman, and Elizabeth F. Loftus. "Juror's Attitudes About Civil Litigation and the Size of Damage Awards." *American University Washington College of Law.* n.d. http://www.wcl.american.edu/journal/lawrev/40/greene.pdf?rd=1 (accessed February 24, 2012).

Green, W. C. *Was it okay for the Japanese to torture our soldiers if the justification.* 25 April 2009. http://www.democraticunderground.com/discuss/duboard.php?az=view_all&address=132x8370430 (accessed March 16, 2012).

Grey, Ian. *Jim Greer, Ex-Florida GOP Chair, Claims Republican Voting Laws Focused On Suppression, Racism.* 26 November 2012.

http://www.huffingtonpost.com/2012/11/26/jim-greer-florida-voting-laws_n_2192802.html (accessed November 27, 2012).

Guarino, Mark. *Chicago registers its 500th homicide of 2012—the highest number since 2008.* 29 December 2012. http://www.csmonitor.com/USA/Society/2012/1229/Chicago-registers-its-500th-homicide-of-2012-the-highest-number-since-2008 (accessed December 29, 2012).

Harkinson, Josh. *21 CEOs With $100 Million Golden Parachutes.* 18 January 2012. http://motherjones.com/mojo/2012/01/executive-pay-100-million-ceo-severance-packages (accessed March 4, 2012).

Harrison, George. *The Beatles—Taxman Lyrics.* 1966. http://www.lyrics007.com/The%20Beatles%20Lyrics/Taxman%20Lyrics.html (accessed April 11, 2013).

Higginbotham, A. Leon, Jr. "An Open Letter to Justice Clarence Thomas from a Federal Judicial Colleague." *University of Pennsylvania Law Review*, January 1992: 1005–1020.

The Holy Bible, King James Version. Matthew 22:21. n.d.

Hudson, Waymon. *Election 2012: Voter ID Laws, Suppression, and Equality.* 20 September 2012. http://www.huffingtonpost.com/waymon-hudson/election-2012-voter-id-laws-suppression-and-equality_b_1898613.html (accessed November 18, 2012).

Huerta, Dolores. *TOGETHER WE WILL END RACISM.* n.d. http://www.now.org/issues/diverse/ending.html (accessed April 10, 2012).

Huffington Post. *CEO-To-Worker Pay Ratio Ballooned 1,000 Percent Since 1950: Report.* 30 April 2013. http://www.huffingtonpost.com/2013/04/30/ceo-to-worker-pay-ratio_n_3184623.html?ref=topbar (accessed April 30, 2013).

———. *Court Cell Phone Ban: Chicago Criminal Court Judge Thinks Ban Could Prevent Witness Murder.* 13 April 2013. http://www.huffingtonpost.com/2013/04/13/court-cell-phone-ban-chic_n_3075891.html (accessed April 13, 2013).

———. *Dan Rather: Corporate Media 'Is In Bed With' Washington.* 20 May 2012. http://www.huffingtonpost.com/2012/05/20/dan-rather-cbs-news-corporate-media_n_1531121.html?ref=topbar (accessed May 20, 2012).

———. *Gallup Poll Finds Confidence In TV News Has Hit A New Low.* 11 July 2012. http://www.huffingtonpost.com/2012/07/11/gallup-poll-confidence-tv-news_n_1664429.html (accessed July 11, 2012).

————. *George Zimmerman's Mother, Gladys Zimmerman, Pens Open Letter On One Year Anniversary Of Son's Arrest.* 11 April 2013. http://www.huffingtonpost.com/2013/04/11/george-zimmermans-mother-open-letter_n_3064028.html (accessed April 11, 2013).

————. *Inauguration Speech: Obama Starts Second Term With Remarks At U.S. Capitol (FULL TRANSCRIPT).* 21 January 2013. http://www.huffingtonpost.com/2013/01/21/inauguration-speech_n_2491757.html (accessed March 27, 2013).

————. *Martin Bashir Compares IRS Attacks On Obama To 'N-Word.'* 5 June 2013. http://www.huffingtonpost.com/2013/06/05/martin-bashir-irs-n-word_n_3392578.html (accessed June 5, 2013).

————. *Supreme Court Poll: Only 44 Percent Of Americans Approve Of The Job The Court Is Doing.* 8 June 2012. http://www.huffingtonpost.com/2012/06/08/supreme-court-poll_n_1580139.html?icid=maing-grid7%7Cmain5%7Cdl6%7Csec3_lnk3%26pLid%3D168202 (accessed June 8, 2012).

————. *Supreme Court Rules On Prop 8.* 26 June 2013. http://www.huffingtonpost.com/2013/06/26/supreme-court-prop-8_n_3434854.html (accessed June 26, 2013).

————. *Tom Brokaw: 'It Is Time To Rethink' White House Correspondents Dinner.* 6 May 2012. http://www.huffingtonpost.com/2012/05/06/tom-brokaw-white-house-correspondents-dinner_n_1489850.html?ncid=edlinkusaolp00000003 (accessed May 20, 2012).

————. *Wedding Banned: Black Couple Told They Can't Wed In Baptist Church.* 27 July 2012. http://www.huffingtonpost.com/2012/07/27/wedding-banned_n_1711201.html?ir=Black+Voices&ref=topbar (accessed July 27, 2012).

Humes, Karen R., Nicolas A. Jones, and Roberto R. Ramirez. *Overview of Race and Hispanic Origen: 2010.* March 2011. http://www.census.gov/prod/cen2010/briefs/c2010br-02.pdf (accessed April 26, 2013).

Hutchison, Earl. *Clarence Thomas's silence on bench is anything but golden.* 14 February 2011. http://www.thegrio.com/politics/clarence-thomas-silence-on-bench-is-anything-but-golden.php (accessed April 30, 2012).

India.Arie. "I Am Not My Hair." 2006.

The Independent Institute. *TAXING CHOICE: The Predatory Politics of Fiscal Discrimination.* n.d. http://www.independent.org/store/book.asp?id=48 (accessed June 17, 2012).

Infoplease. *Life Expectancy at Birth by Race and Sex, 1930–2010.* n.d. http://www.infoplease.com/ipa/A0005148.html (accessed March 4, 2012).

———. *National Voter Turnout in Federal Elections: 1960–2010.* 2011. http://www.infoplease.com/ipa/A0781453.html (accessed February 17, 2012).

Jefferson, Thomas. *Thomas Jefferson to Edward Carrington.* 16 January 1787. http://press-pubs.uchicago.edu/founders/documents/amendI_speechs8.html (accessed July 11, 2012).

Jeffries, Fran, and Wayne Washington. *Paula Deen Scandal Continues As Employees Tell Rainbow/PUSH Coalition Of Alleged Discrimination.* 23 June 2013. http://www.huffingtonpost.com/2013/06/23/paula-deen-scandal-continues-employees-tell-rainbow-push-alleged-discrimination_n_3484607.html (accessed June 30, 2013).

John F. Kennedy Presidential Library and Museum. *Ready Reference: John F. Kennedy Quotations.* n.d. http://www.jfklibrary.org/Research/Research-Aids/Ready-Reference/JFK-Quotations.aspx (accessed October 4, 2013).

Johnson, Luke. *Clarence Thomas Compares Affirmative Action To Slavery, Segregation In Opinion.* 24 June 2013. http://www.huffingtonpost.com/2013/06/24/clarence-thomas-affirmative-action_n_3491433.html (accessed June 24, 2013).

Jones, Jeffrey M. *Politics: Americans Renew Call for Third Party.* 17 September 2010. http://www.gallup.com/poll/143051/americans-renew-call-third-party.aspx (accessed March 15, 2012).

Jones, Sarah. *The Mind-blowing Hypocrisy of John McCain: WMD Lie is Good, Repeating Intelligence is Bad.* 15 November 2012. http://www.politicususa.com/mindblowing-hypocrisy-john-mccain-wmd-lie-good-repeating-intelligence-bad.html (accessed November 15, 2012).

Katz, Celeste. *Curbing Gun Violence Takes Center Stage In 2013 State Of The Union Address.* 13 February 2013. http://www.nydailynews.com/blogs/dailypolitics/2013/02/curbing-gun-violence-takes-center-stage-in-2013-state-of-the-union-address (accessed March 27, 2013).

Kimble, Julian. *Georgia Man Places Racist Sign in Front of Bar.* 10 May 2012. http://www.complex.com/city-guide/2012/05/georgia-man-places-racist-sign-in-front-of-bar (accessed July 24, 2012).

Klusendorf, Scott. *How to Defend Your Pro-Life Views in 5 Minutes or Less.* n.d. http://www.prolifetraining.com/FiveMinute1.asp (accessed August 20, 2012).

Knowles, John. *Warfare.* 12 March 2002. http://www.pcmag.com/article2/0,2817,509,00.asp (accessed July 25, 2012).

Kois, Dan, and Chris Kirk. *How Many People Have Been Killed by Guns Since Newtown?* 28 March 2013. http://www.slate.com/articles/news_and_politics/crime/2012/12/gun_death_tally_every_american_gun_death_since_newtown_sandy_hook_shooting.html (accessed June 30, 2013).

Lad, Kashmira. *Pros and Cons of Mass Media.* n.d. http://www.buzzle.com/articles/pros-and-cons-of-mass-media.html (accessed March 22, 2012).

Law and Order [Episode: "Bronx Cheer"]. Directed by Richard Dobbs. Performed by Sam Waterston and Keith David. 2001.

Law and Order [Episode: "Thinking Makes It So"]. Directed by Tony Goldwyn. Performed by Sam Waterston. 2006.

The 'Lectric Law Library. *Tort.* n.d. http://www.lectlaw.com/def2/t032.htm (accessed February 24, 2012).

Legal Information Institute. *Sixth Amendment.* n.d. http://www.law.cornell.edu/constitution/sixth_amendment (accessed July 22, 2012).

Library of Congress. *Brown v. Board at Fifty: "With an Even Hand."* n.d. http://www.loc.gov/exhibits/brown/brown-brown.html (accessed July 19, 2013).

Linder, Doug. *The Right To Privacy.* n.d. http://law2.umkc.edu/faculty/projects/ftrials/conlaw/rightofprivacy.html (accessed February 20, 2012).

———. *The Supreme Court in the American System of Government.* 2012. http://law2.umkc.edu/faculty/projects/ftrials/conlaw/supremecourtintro.html (accessed February 19, 2012).

Liptak, Adam. *Supreme Court Strikes Down Key Part of Voting Rights Act.* 25 June 2013. http://www.nytimes.com/2013/06/26/us/supreme-court-ruling.html?_r=0 (accessed June 25, 2013).

Luhby, Tami. *Worsening Wealth Inequality by Race.* 21 June 2012. http://money.cnn.com/2012/06/21/news/economy/wealth-gap-race/index.htm?iid=HP_MPM (accessed June 22, 2012).

Malcolm-X.org. *Quotations.* n.d. http://www.malcolm-x.org/quotes.htm (accessed March 5, 2013).

McNamara, Robert. *The Election of 1828 Was Marked By Dirty Tactics.* n.d. http://history1800s.about.com/od/leaders/a/electionof1828.htm (accessed March 27, 2013).

Meyer, Carlton. *Tenured Flag Officers.* n.d. http://www.g2mil.com/tenured.htm (accessed February 25, 2013).

Monday Mornings: "Episode 2." Directed by Bill D'Elia. Performed by TNT. 2013.

Morales, Lymari. *Gallup Politics.* 15 December 2011. http://www.gallup.com/poll/151556/fewer-americans-divided-haves-nots.aspx (accessed March 2, 2012).

MSNBC.com. *Jury awards record $150 billion payout to family of burned child.* 2011. http://www.msnbc.msn.com/id/45761980/ns/us_news-crime_and_courts/t/jury-awards-record-billion-payout-family-burned-child/ (accessed February 24, 2012).

Network. Directed by Sidney Lumet. Performed by Peter Finch. 1976.

Niebuhr, Reinhold. *The Serenity Prayer.* 1943. http://www.cptryon.org/prayer/special/serenity.html (accessed July 10, 2012).

Nittle, Nadra Kareem. *Definition of Colorism.* n.d. http://racerelations.about.com/od/understandingrac1/g/definitionofcolorism.htm (accessed December 10, 2012).

Patterson, Orlando. *Sunday Book Review.* 17 June 2007. http://www.nytimes.com/2007/06/17/books/review/Patterson-t.html?pagewanted=all (accessed April 30, 2012).

Obama, Barack. *2009 Executive Orders Disposition Tables / Barack Obama 2009.* 22 January 2009. http://www.archives.gov/federal-register/executive-orders/2009-obama.html (accessed February 24, 2012).

Pearson, Richard. *Former Ala. Gov. George C. Wallace Dies.* September 14, 1998. http://www.washingtonpost.com/wp-srv/politics/daily/sept98/wallace.htm (accessed August 27, 2013).

The Pew Forum on Religion and Public Life. *U.S. Religious Landscape Survey.* 2007. http://religions.pewforum.org/reports# (accessed February 27, 2012).

———. *2011 Executive Orders Disposition Tables / Barack Obama 2011.* 7 March 2011. http://www.archives.gov/federal-register/executive-orders/2011.html (accessed February 24, 2012).

PolitiFact.com. *PBS commentator Mark Shields says more killed by guns since '68 than in all U.S. wars.* January 18, 2013. http://www.politifact.com/truth-o-meter/statements/2013/jan/18/mark-shields/pbs-commentator-mark-shields-says-more-killed-guns/ (accessed September 19, 2013).

Prologue Magazine. Kennedy Library Observes Fortieth Anniversary of Missile Crisis. 2002. http://www.archives.gov/publications/prologue/2002/fall/cuban-missiles.html (accessed September 17, 2012).

The Quotations Page. *Quotation by Authors (George W. Bush).* n.d. http://www.quotationspage.com/quotes/George_W._Bush (accessed May 20, 2013).

QuotationsBook. *Quotes About Force.* n.d. http://quotationsbook.com/quotes/tag/force/ (accessed September 18, 2012).

Quotes. *Gen. H. Norman Schwarzkopf.* n.d. http://www.quotes.net/quote/8951 (accessed February 5, 2013).

Recktenwald, William. *922 Homicides Made 1991 Year To Forget.* 1 January 1992. http://articles.chicagotribune.com/1992-01-01/news/9201010135_1_homicide-victim-drug-trafficking-killed (accessed December 31, 2012).

Repa, Barbara. *Federal Labor Laws.* n.d. http://www.nolo.com/legal-encyclopedia/free-books/employee-rights-book/chapter15-2.html (accessed April 14, 2013).

Rojas, Marcela. *Biden praises cadets at West Point commencement.* 27 June 2012. http://www.usatoday.com/news/military/story/2012-05-27/biden-west-point-commencement/55226904/1 (accessed July 22, 2012).

Rothman, Noah. *Cornell West On Sandy Hook: 'We Can't Just Shed Tears For Those On The Vanilla Side Of Town.'* 27 December 2012. http://www.mediaite.com/online/cornell-west-on-sandy-hook-we-cant-just-shed-tears-for-those-on-the-vanilla-side-of-town/ (accessed December 29, 2012).

Scalia, Antonin, and Clarence Thomas. *Supreme Court of the United States in Re Troy Anthony Davis.* 17 August 2009. http://www.supremecourt.gov/opinions/08pdf/08-1443Scalia.pdf (accessed July 12, 2012).

The Scent of a Woman. Directed by Martin Brest. Performed by Al Pacino. 1992.

Schneider, Mike, and Kyle Hightower. *Trayvon Martin Friend, Rachel Jeantel, Returns To Stand At George Zimmerman Trial.* 27 June 2013. http://www.huffingtonpost.com/2013/06/27/trayvon-martin-rachel-jeantel-george-zimmerman-trial_n_3509141.html (accessed July 12, 2013).

Serwer, Adam. *Rachel Jeantel and Juror B37: 2 Women, 2 Stories.* 19 July 2013. http://www.theroot.com/buzz/rachel-jeantel-and-juror-b37-2-women-2-stories (accessed July 25, 2013).

Skousen, W. Cleon. "The Making of America." In *The Making of America*, by W. Cleon Skousen, 239. National Center for Constitutional Studies, 1986.

Spagat, Elliot. *Border Patrol Gets First New Strategy In 8 Years.* 8 May 2012. http://www.huffingtonpost.com/2012/05/08/border-patrol-gets-first-_0_n_1499599.html (accessed May 8, 2012).

Standard Operating Procedure. Directed by Errol Morris. Performed by ENCORE Drama. 2013.

Standler, Ronald B. *Differences between Civil and Criminal Law in the USA.* 19 October 2002. http://www.rbs2.com/cc.htm#anchor222222 (accessed February 23, 2012).

Star-Ledger Continuous News Desk. *Dressing fake monkey in anti-Obama T-shirt was not racist move, ex-Cedar Grove councilman says.* 8 August 2012. http://www.nj.com/news/index.ssf/2012/08/dressing_fake_monkey_in_anti-o.html (accessed August 9, 2012).

Starr, Barbara. *Scathing message sent to Navy SEALs on discussing secret work.* 4 September 2012. http://wtvr.com/2012/09/04/scathing-message-sent-to-navy-seals-on-discussing-secret-work/ (accessed September 4, 2012).

Steiner, Craig. *The Clinton Surplus Myth.* 22 August 2011. http://finance.townhall.com/columnists/craigsteiner/2011/08/22/the_clinton_surplus_myth/page/full/ (accessed September 4, 2012).

Suiter, Dale R. *Duty—Honor—Country.* 5 April 2011. http://www.veteranstoday.com/2011/04/05/duty-honor-country/ (accessed February 24, 2013).

Superville, Darlene. *Obama: Voting Rights Act Provision Should Be Kept.* 22 February 2013. http://www.huffingtonpost.com/2013/02/22/obama-voting-rights-_n_2741191.html (accessed February 22, 2013).

Swartz, Tracy. *Tracking Homicides in Chicago.* n.d. http://homicides.redeyechicago.com/ (accessed January 16, 2013).

Taylor, Jill Bolte. *Does Our Planet Need a Stroke of Insight?* 4 January 2013. http://www.huffingtonpost.com/dr-jill-bolte-taylor/neuroscience_

b_2404554.html?icid=maing-grid7%7Cmain5%7Cdl4%7Csec1_ lnk1%26pLid%3D253014 (accessed January 5, 2013).

Tennyson, Sir Alfred Lord. *The Charge of the Light Brigade.* n.d. http:// poetry.eserver.org/light-brigade.html (accessed July 22, 2012).

The Tenth Amendment Center. *Less Democrat—Less Republican—More Constitution.* 20 June 2013.

Thomas, Edwin. *What Is Social Security Tax Used for?* n.d. http:// www.ehow.com/about_5212871_social-security-tax-used-for_.html (accessed February 17, 2012).

Thompson, Hunter S. *Hunter S. Thompson Quotes.* n.d. http://www. goodreads.com/quotes/47188-life-should-not-be-a-journey-to-the-grave-with (accessed April 7, 2013).

TMZ. *Michael Clarke Duncan's Tomb Vandalized by Racist ... Says Family.* 24 May 2013. http://www.tmz.com/2013/05/24/michael-clarke-duncan-gravesite-vandalized-with-racist-figure/ (accessed May 24, 2013).

Troutt, David Dante. *Voting Rights: Scalia v. minority protection.* 5 March 2013. http://blogs.reuters.com/great-debate/2013/03/05/voting-rights-scalia-v-minority-protection/ (accessed March 5, 2013).

The Tuskegee Airmen. Directed by Robert Markowitz. Performed by Andre Braugher. 1995.

TVNewser. *Court TV Founder Trashes Nancy Grace.* 2011. http://www. tvweek.com/blogs/tvbizwire/2011/07/court-tv-founder-trashes-nancy. php (accessed July 22, 2012).

United States Holocaust Memorial Museum. *Martin Niemöller: "First they came for the Socialists ...".* n.d. http://www.ushmm.org/wlc/en/ article.php?ModuleId=10007392 (accessed May 16, 2012).

Urban Dictionary. *Cablinasian.* n.d. http://www.urbandictionary.com/ define.php?term=Cablinasian (accessed December 10, 2012).

US Immigration Support. *Wet-Foot Dry-Foot Policy.* n.d. http://www. usimmigrationsupport.org/wetfoot-dryfoot.html (accessed February 28, 2012).

US Legal. *Blackmail Law & Legal Definition.* n.d. http://definitions. uslegal.com/b/blackmail (accessed February 23, 2012).

Vasilogambros, Matt and Huisenga, Sarah. *Romney Blasts Obama on Cairo Embassy Statement of 'Sympathy.'* 11 September 2012. http://www.nationaljournal.com/2012-presidential-campaign/

romney-blasts-obama-on-cairo-embassy-statement-of-sympathy—20120911 (accessed October 15, 2012).

Vyan. *George Lucas "Red Tails" gives Tuskegee Airmen the Rocking War Movie they Deserve.* 19 January 2012. http://www.dailykos.com/story/2012/01/19/1056245/-George-Lucas-Red-Tails-gives-Tuskegee-Airmen-the-Rocking-War-Movie-they-Deserve (accessed March 31, 2013).

Wall Street. Directed by Oliver Stone. Performed by Michael Douglas. 1987.

Walsh, Joan. *The real story of the shutdown: 50 years of GOP race-baiting.* October 1, 2013. http://www.salon.com/2013/10/01/the_real_story_of_the_shutdown_50_years_of_gop_race_baiting/ (accessed October 1, 2013).

Washington Post. Text of President Obama's May 23 speech on national security (full transcript). 23 May 2013. http://www.washingtonpost.com/politics/president-obamas-may-23-speech-on-national-security-as-prepared-for-delivery/2013/05/23/02c35e30-c3b8-11e2-9fe2-6ee52d0eb7c1_story.html (accessed May 24, 2013).

Western Washington University. *America's Rich Get Richer.* February 2012. http://hope.journ.wwu.edu/tpilgrim/j190/richgetricher.html (accessed March 2, 2012).

Whelan, Ed. *District of Columbia v. Heller: Scalia's Majority Opinion.* 26 June 2008. http://www.nationalreview.com/bench-memos/50849/district-columbia-v-heller-scalias-majority-opinion/ed-whelan (accessed January 31, 2013).

Who is Black in America? Performed by CNN and Soledad O'Brien. 2012.

WikiAnswers *Why are US Supreme Court justices appointed for life?* n.d. http://wiki.answers.com/Q/Why_are_US_Supreme_Court_justices_appointed_for_life (accessed February 20, 2012).

Wikipedia, the free encyclopedia. *40 Acres and a Mule.* n.d. http://en.wikipedia.org/wiki/40_acres_and_a_mule (accessed June 22, 2012).

———. *Arnaud Amalric.* n.d. http://en.wikipedia.org/wiki/Arnaud_Amalric (accessed August 10, 2012).

———. *Ash Heap of History.* n.d. http://en.wikipedia.org/wiki/Ash_heap_of_history (accessed September 26, 2012).

———. *Black Billionaires.* n.d. http://en.wikipedia.org/wiki/Black_billionaires (accessed June 22, 2012).

———. *Damages.* n.d. http://en.wikipedia.org/wiki/Damages (accessed February 24, 2012).

———. *Defense of Marriage Act.* n.d. http://en.wikipedia.org/wiki/Defense_of_Marriage_Act (accessed May 9, 2012).

———. *Discrimination based on skin color.* n.d. http://en.wikipedia.org/wiki/Discrimination_based_on_skin_color (accessed December 11, 2012).

———. *Gun Violence in the United States.* n.d. http://en.wikipedia.org/wiki/Gun_violence_in_the_United_States#Violent_crime_related_to_guns (accessed December 27, 2012).

———. *List of school shootings in the United States.* n.d. http://en.wikipedia.org/wiki/List_of_school_shootings_in_the_United_States (accessed December 27, 2012).

———. *Media Bias in the United States.* n.d. http://en.wikipedia.org/wiki/Media_bias_in_the_United_States (accessed May 21, 2012).

———. *Münchausen Syndrome By Proxy.* n.d. http://en.wikipedia.org/wiki/M%C3%BCnchausen_syndrome_by_proxy (accessed December 2, 2012).

———. *National Rifle Association.* n.d. https://en.wikipedia.org/wiki/National_Rifle_Association (accessed May 5, 2013).

———. *Natural-Born-Citizen Clause of the U.S. Constitution.* n.d. http://en.wikipedia.org/wiki/Natural-born-citizen_clause_of_the_U.S._Constitution (accessed February 26, 2012).

———. *The New Colossus.* n.d. http://en.wikipedia.org/wiki/The_New_Colossus (accessed July 23, 2012).

———. *Nigger.* n.d. http://en.wikipedia.org/wiki/Nigger (accessed July 1, 2013).

———. *Roe v. Wade.* n.d. http://en.wikipedia.org/wiki/Roe_v._Wade (accessed August 22, 2012).

———. *Si vis pacem, para bellum.* n.d. http://en.wikipedia.org/wiki/Si_vis_pacem,_para_bellum (accessed February 28, 2013).

———. *Tailhook Scandal.* n.d. http://en.wikipedia.org/wiki/Tailhook_scandal (accessed February 25, 2013).

———. *Tawana Brawley Rape Allegations.* n.d. http://en.wikipedia.org/wiki/Tawana_Brawley_rape_allegations#Public_response (accessed February 20, 2012).

———. *Time, Inc. v. Hill.* n.d. http://en.wikipedia.org/wiki/Time,_Inc._v._Hill (accessed February 20, 2012).

————. *Title II Weapons*. n.d. http://en.wikipedia.org/wiki/Title_II_ weapons (accessed May 5, 2013).

————. *Tort Reform*. n.d. http://en.wikipedia.org/wiki/Tort_reform (accessed February 20, 2012).

————. *Treaty on the Non-Proliferation of Nuclear Weapons*. n.d. http://en.wikipedia.org/wiki/Treaty_on_the_Non-Proliferation_of_ Nuclear_Weapons (accessed September 22, 2012).

————. *Trebel Damages*. n.d. http://en.wikipedia.org/wiki/Treble_ damages (accessed February 25, 2012).

————. *Unique Identification Authority of India*. n.d. http:// en.wikipedia.org/wiki/Unique_Identification_Authority_of_India (accessed July 3, 2012).

————. *United Nations Security Council and the Iraq War*. n.d. http:// en.wikipedia.org/wiki/United_Nations_Security_Council_and_the_ Iraq_War (accessed March 18, 2012).

————. *Walter Cronkite*. n.d. http://en.wikipedia.org/wiki/Walter_Cronkite (accessed May 28, 2012).

Wikiquote. *Herman Cain*. 8 October 2011. http://en.wikiquote.org/wiki/ Herman_Cain (accessed July 31, 2012).

————. *Hubert Humphrey*. n.d. http://en.wikiquote.org/wiki/Hubert_ Humphrey (accessed July 22, 2012).

————. *Sun Tzu*. n.d. http://en.wikiquote.org/wiki/Sun_Tzu (accessed July 22, 2012).

WildBranch Ministry. "The War Scroll." WildBranch Ministry. n.d. www. wildbranch.org/teachings/ . . . /The%20War%20Scroll.ppt (accessed August 11, 2012).

Wile, Rob. *Duke Energy CEO to Get $44 Million in Severance for 3 Days of Work*. 6 July 2012. http://www.dailyfinance.com/2012/07/06/ duke-energy-ceo-to-get-44-million-in-severance-for-3-days-of-wo/ (accessed July 6, 2012).

Wing, Nick. *Gabrielle Giffords Eviscerates Senators After Vote To Reject Gun Background Checks Amendment*. 17 April 2013. http://www. huffingtonpost.com/2013/04/17/gabrielle-giffords-gun-vote_n_3103876. html?ref=topbar (accessed April 18, 2013).

Wiseman, Paul. *U.S. Economic Recovery Is Weakest Since World War II*. 15 August 2012. http://www.huffingtonpost.com/2012/08/15/us- economic-recovery-weak_n_1783065.html (accessed August 15, 2012).

Wood, Sarah. *Mitt Romney: I Can Relate To Black People, My Ancestors Once Owned Slaves.* 13 March 2012. http://www.freewoodpost.com/2012/03/13/mitt-romney-i-can-relate-to-black-people-my-ancestors-once-owned-slaves/ (accessed May 10, 2012).

World of NEWSNINJA2012. *Cornel West on Sandy Hook Tragedy: "We can't just shed tears for those on the vanilla side of town."* 28 December 2012. http://newsninja2012.com/cornel-west-on-sandy-hook-tragedy-we-cant-just-shed-tears-for-those-on-the-vanilla-side-of-town/#axzz2HDPSQpoB (accessed January 6, 2013).

Young, Tomas. *The Last Letter.* March 2013. http://www.truthdig.com/dig/item/the_last_letter_20130318/ (accessed March 19, 2013).

YouTube. *Bin Laden letters warn against Muslim deaths.* 4 May 2012. http://www.youtube.com/watch?v=yxc9nfhyj0I (accessed April 8, 2013).

———. *MALCOLM X: We are Africans who were kidnapped and brought to America.* 30 June 2006. http://www.youtube.com/watch?v=xDXPpfGAZrU (accessed July 10, 2012).